THOMAS COLE'S PAINTINGS OF EDEN

Thomas Cole's Paintings of Eden

BY FRANKLIN KELLY

WITH TECHNICAL NOTES BY CLAIRE M. BARRY

AMON CARTER MUSEUM

FORT WORTH, TEXAS

Designed by Jerry Kelly and Lissa Dodington
Printed and bound by The Stinehour Press, Lunenburg, Vermont

CATALOGING-IN-PUBLICATION DATA

Kelly, Franklin.
Thomas Cole's paintings of Eden / by Franklin Kelly; with technical notes by Claire M. Barry
p. cm.
Exhibition catalog.
Includes bibliographical references (p. 69).
1. Cole, Thomas, 1801–1848--Exhibitions. 2. Eden in art--Exhibitions. 3. Artists' preparatory studies--United States--Exhibitions. I. Barry, Claire M. II. Title.
ND237.C6A4 1994a 94-23139
759.13--dc20 CIP

ISBN 0-88360-083-8

Cover: Thomas Cole, *The Garden of Eden*, oil on canvas, 1828

Contents

Director's Foreword

Thomas Cole's Paintings of Eden is the second in a series of small, in-depth exhibitions that focus on single major works of art in the Amon Carter Museum's collection. The first, devoted to Martin Johnson Heade's *Thunder Storm on Narragansett Bay*, opened at the Museum in February 1994 and subsequently traveled to the Shelburne Museum, Shelburne, Vermont, and The Metropolitan Museum of Art, New York. A third focus exhibition, scheduled for 1996, will be dedicated to *The Swimming Hole* by Thomas Eakins.

It was the Museum's acquisition of *The Garden of Eden* in 1990 that prompted this series. To celebrate the discovery of Thomas Cole's painting, which had been lost from public view for over 160 years, Doreen Bolger, at that time Curator of Paintings and Sculpture at the Amon Carter Museum, proposed the projects as visual reports or dossiers built around a single work or a small group of closely related works of great artistic merit and historical interest. *The Garden* and its dramatic pendant, *Expulsion from the Garden of Eden*, have not been seen together since 1829. Presenting these two works with Cole's related sketches gives visitors to this exhibition an opportunity never available before, and affords a greater understanding and appreciation for Cole's creative process and methods.

The small-scale show also takes into account the interests of museum goers. Instead of becoming overwhelmed by "blockbuster" exhibitions, visitors will have an opportunity for contemplation and time to savor the many visual delights. Certainly, this publication will also have lasting value to art historians and visitors to the Amon Carter Museum well after the exhibition has closed.

Multiple collaborations have contributed to the success of this project. First, I wish to extend sincere appreciation to Franklin Kelly, Curator of American and British Paintings at the National Gallery of Art, who has provided us with an informative and engaging interpretation of Thomas Cole's paintings of Eden. It is always a pleasure to work with him. His impeccable research and timely submission of materials are an editor's delight. Fronia W. Simpson, who edited the manuscript with her usual care and enthusiasm, was a welcome addition to our project team. Assistant Curator Sarah Cash has overseen the myriad details for this exhibition and catalogue in her usual thorough manner. Claire M. Barry, Chief Conservator in the Museum's painting conservation program, sponsored jointly with the Kimbell Art Museum, restored *The Garden of Eden* to its current beautiful state and prepared the extensive technical notes for this catalogue. In her restoration she worked closely with Doreen Bolger, now Director, Museum of Art, Rhode Island School of Design. Allison Perkins, Education Director at the Amon Carter Museum, skillfully coordinated and oversaw the development of imaginative programs and materials integral to each focus exhibition. As with all our publication projects, we turned to Nancy Stevens and Jane Posey for their able assistance in seeing the publication through to completion, and to our talented photographers, Rynda Lemke and Steven Watson, for providing the exquisite illustrations. Finally, to registrars Melissa Thompson and Julie Causey, we extend our appreciation for overseeing the safe transport of precious loans.

Lenders to the exhibition have forfeited their enjoyment of important works by Cole in the interest of our greater understanding of the artist and his appealing and provocative pictures. We are indebted to our colleagues and their visitors at The Detroit Institute of Arts; The Metropolitan Museum of Art; Museum of Fine Arts, Boston; the National Gallery of Art; the New York Public Library; the New York State Library, Albany; and the Thyssen-Bornemisza Collection. Without their cooperation this project could not have been completed successfully.

We also gratefully acknowledge The Henry Luce Foundation, Inc., and its board of directors, who in 1991 awarded the Museum a grant for this and the two other exhibitions in the series. This generous gift has resulted not only in a beautiful and informative installation but also in the development of new ways to interpret the collection of the Amon Carter Museum. In this effort, as in so many we have undertaken, we have also enjoyed the support of the National Endowment for the Arts and the National Endowment for the Humanities, federal agencies. The Museum was also fortunate to receive support for the exhibition and its education programs from the Texas Committee for the Humanities, a state program of the National Endowment for the Humanities; and the Texas Commission on the Arts, a state agency.

JAN KEENE MUHLERT
Director
Amon Carter Museum

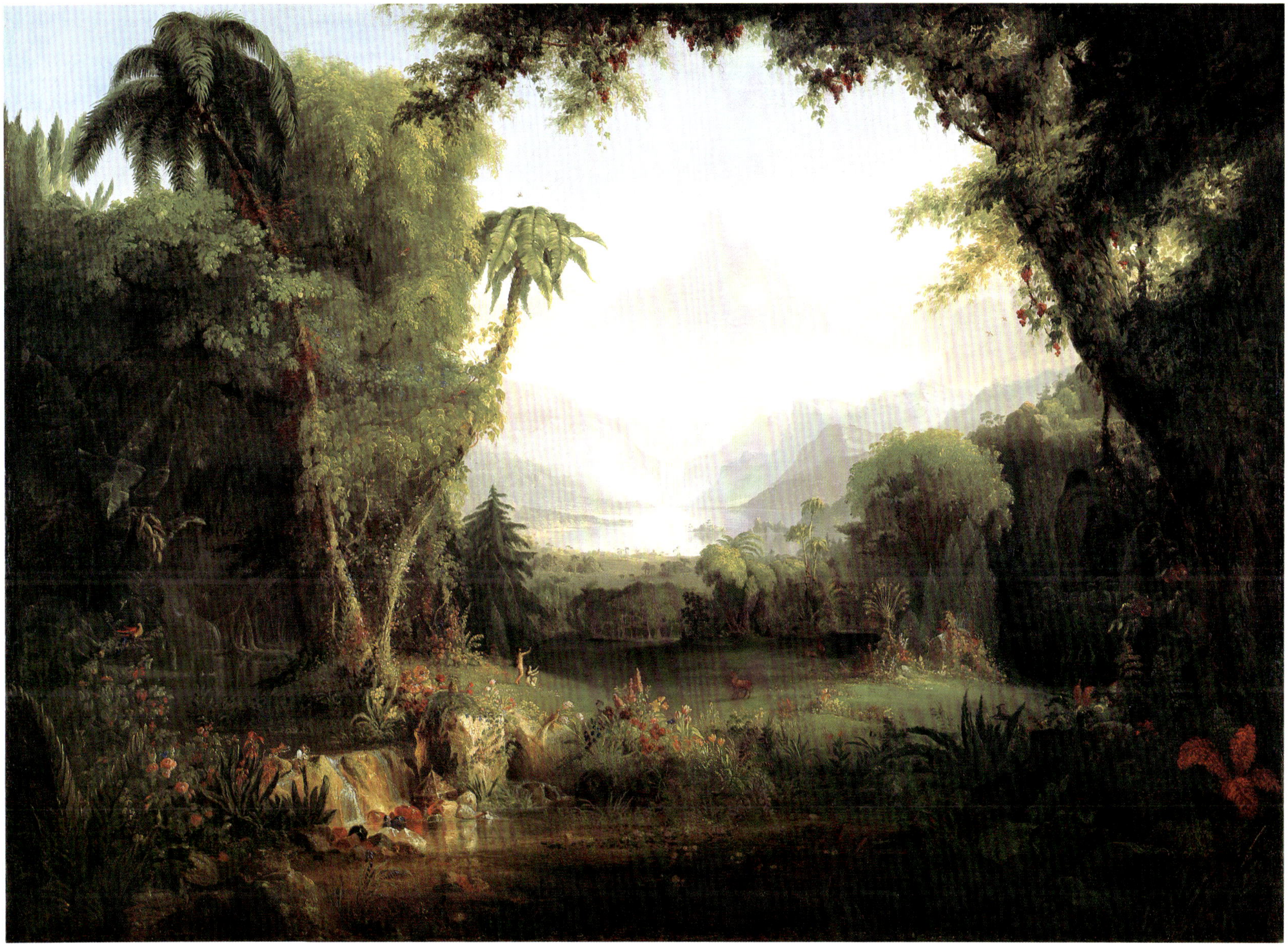

Plate 1. Thomas Cole, *The Garden of Eden*, oil on canvas, 1828, 38½ x 52¾ in., Amon Carter Museum, Fort Worth

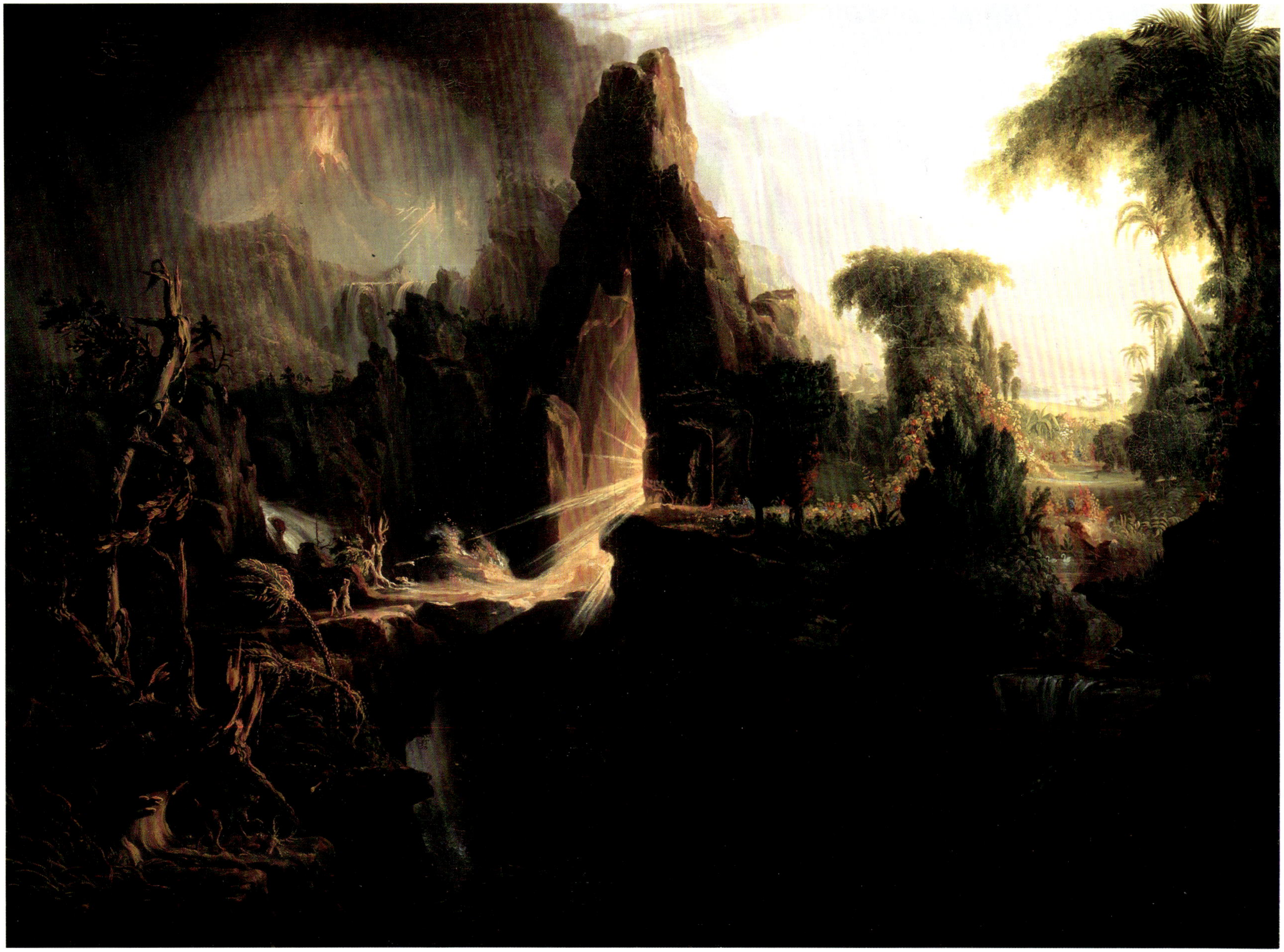

Plate 2. Thomas Cole, *Expulsion from the Garden of Eden*, oil on canvas, 1828, 39 x 54 in., Museum of Fine Arts, Boston, M. & M. Karolik Collection

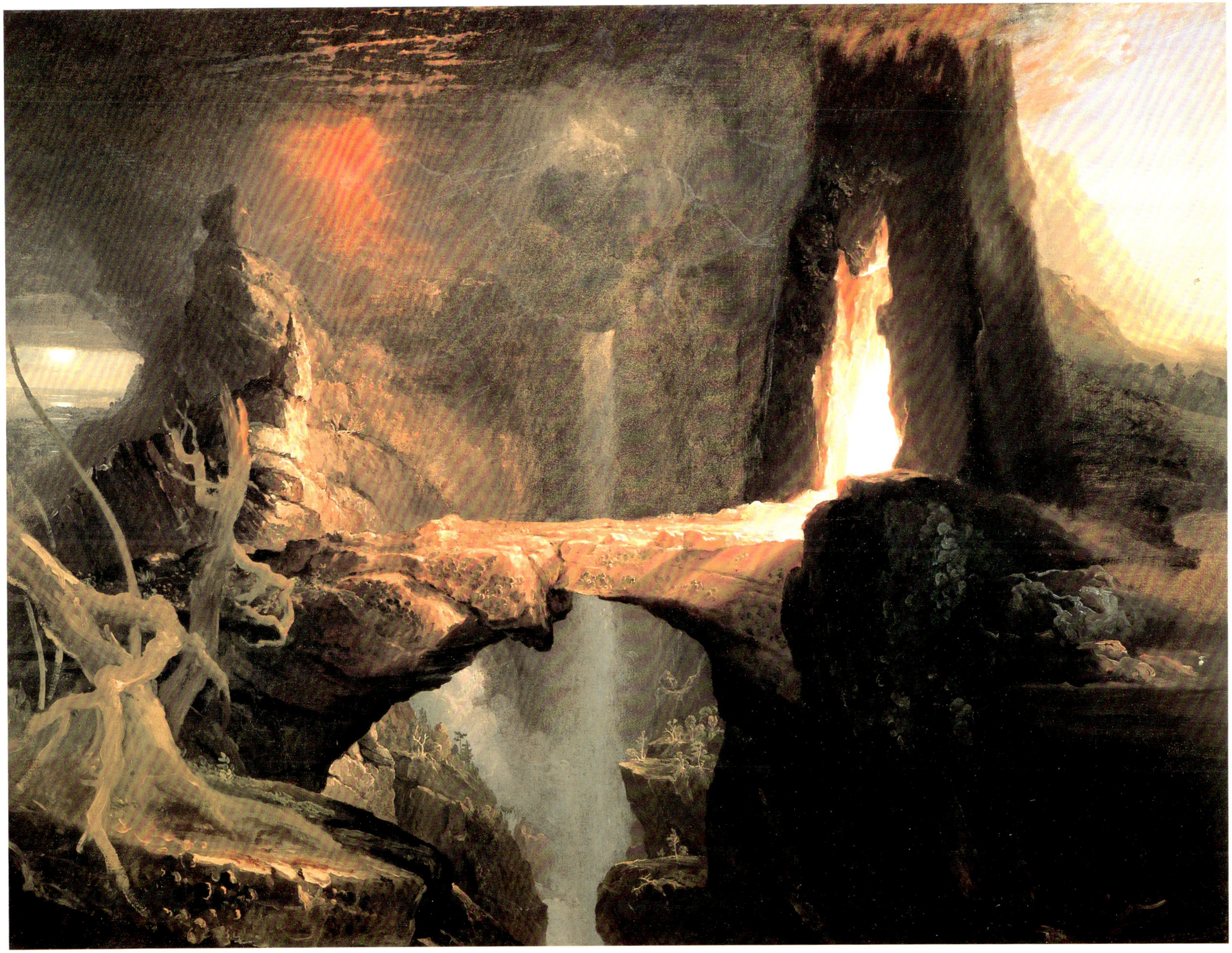

Plate 3. Thomas Cole, *The Expulsion – Moon and Firelight*, oil on canvas, c. 1827/28, 36 x $48\frac{1}{16}$ in., All Rights Reserved. © Fundacion Coleccion Thyssen-Bornemisza, Madrid

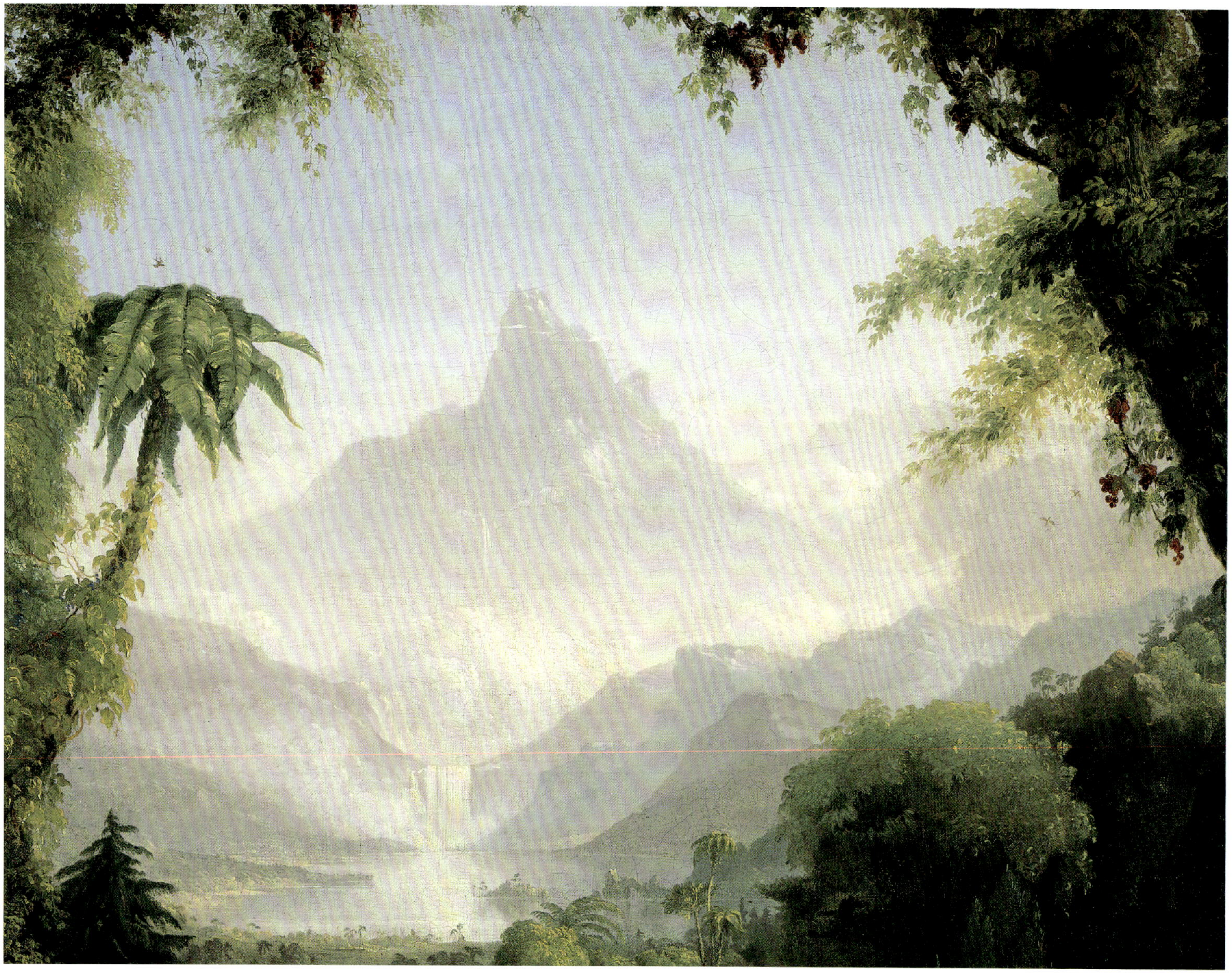

Plate 4. Detail of *The Garden of Eden*

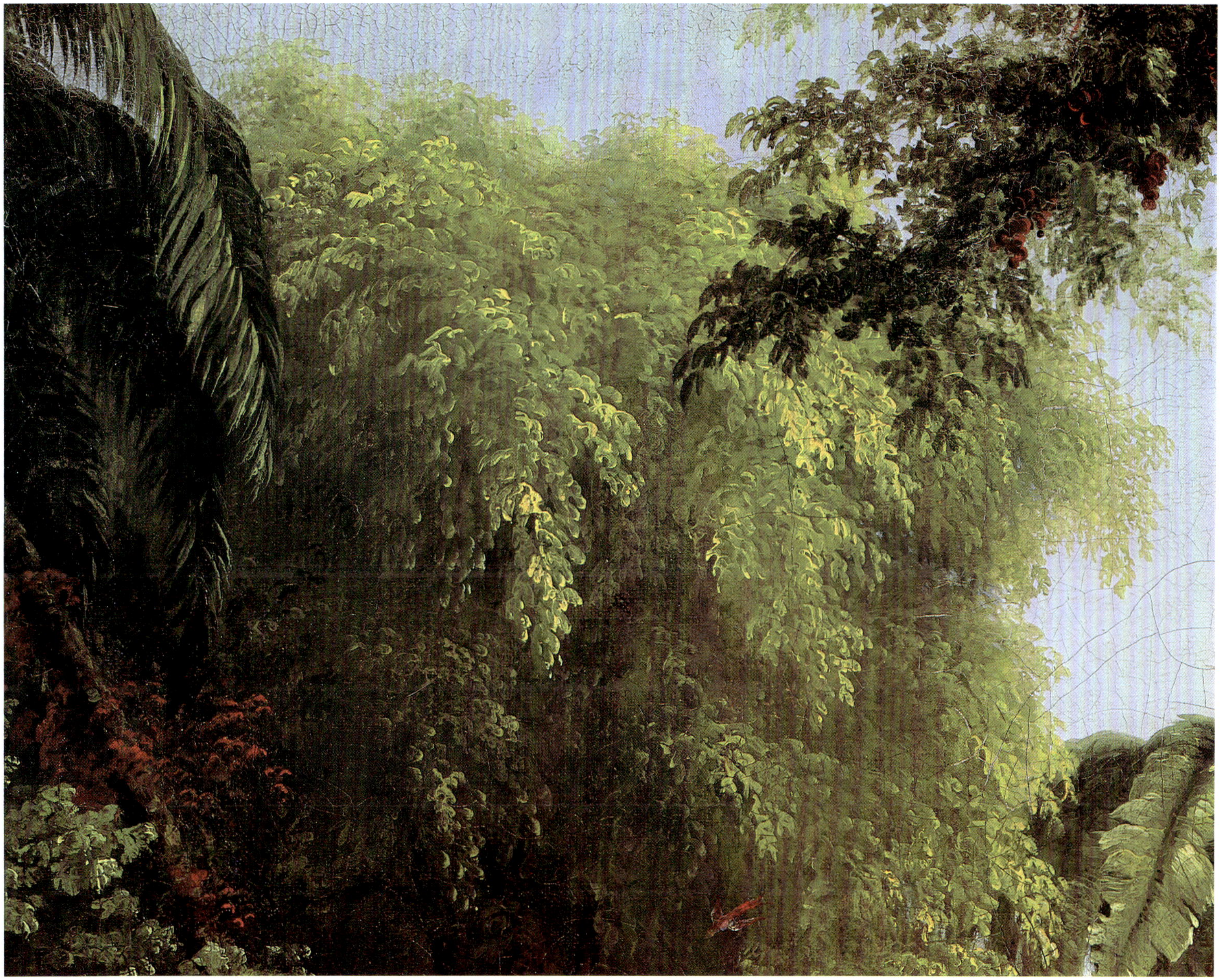

Plate 5. Detail of *The Garden of Eden*

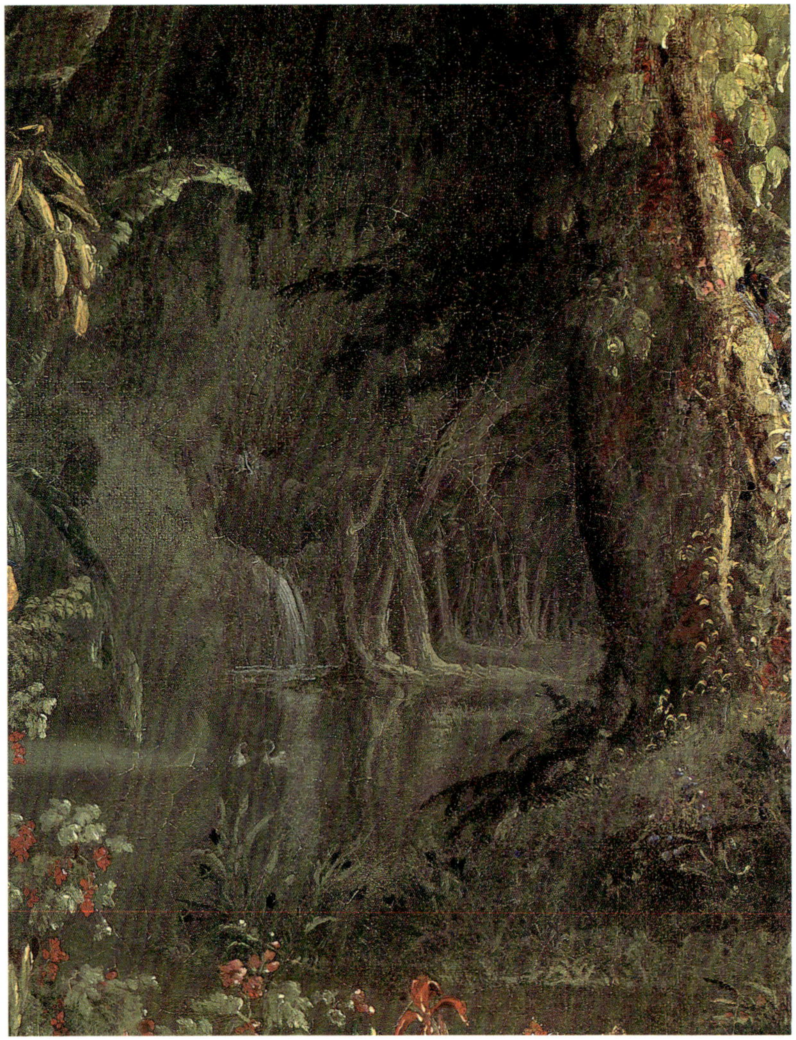

Plate 6. Detail of *The Garden of Eden*

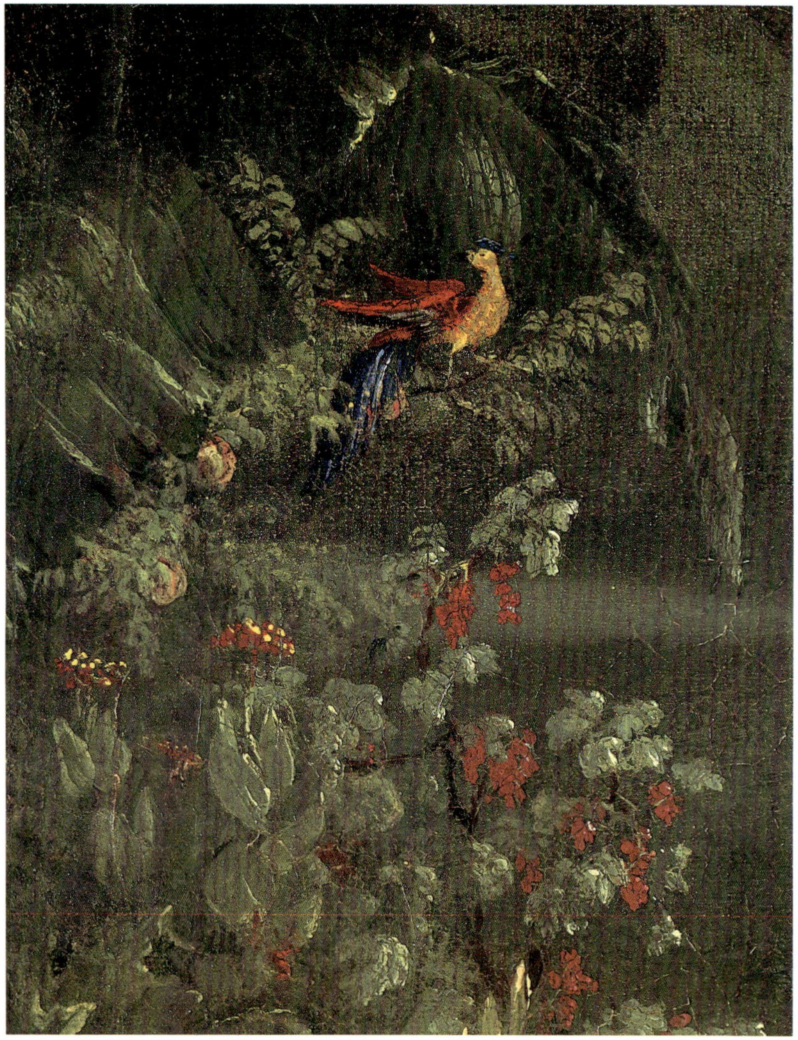

Plate 7. Detail of *The Garden of Eden*

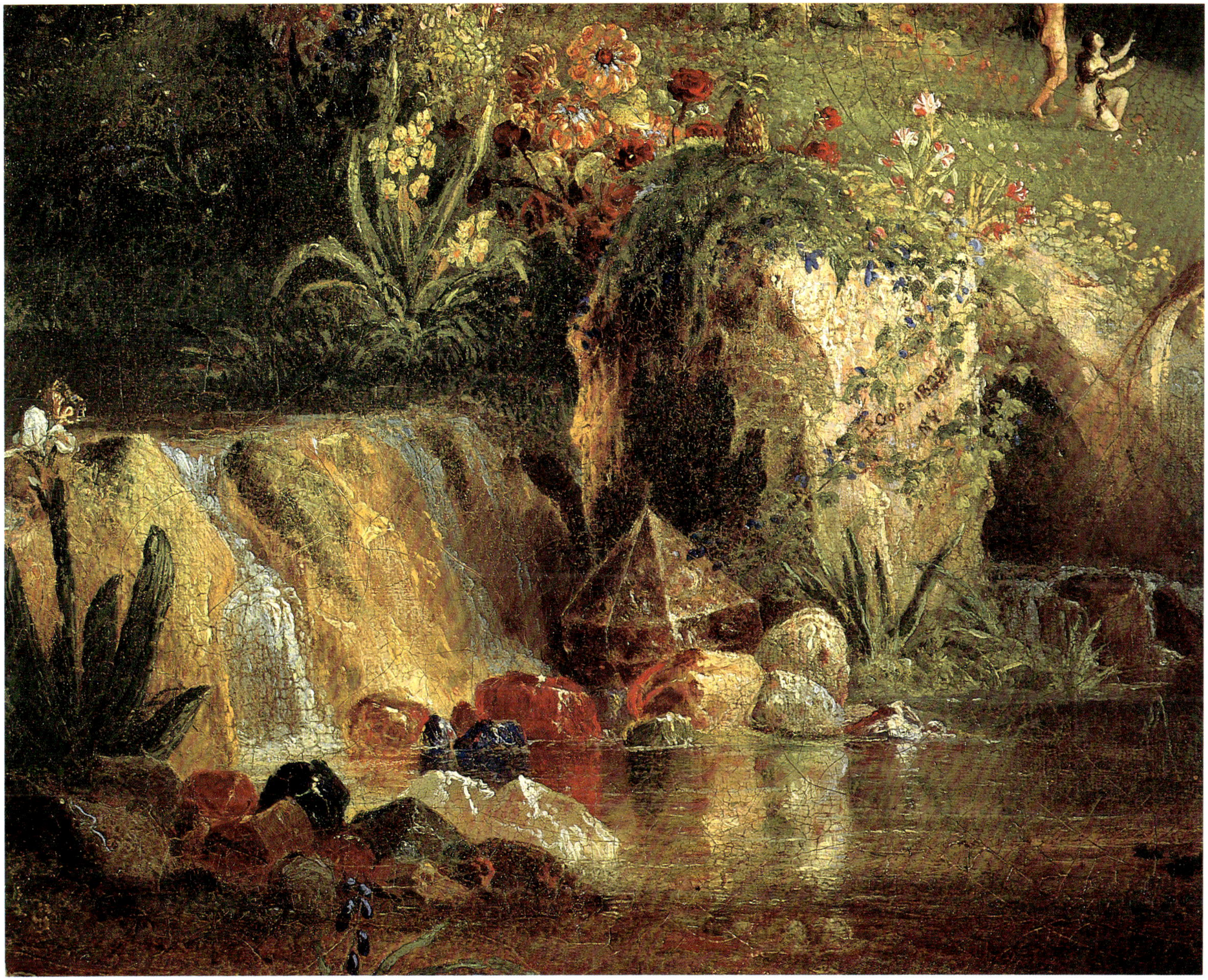

Plate 8. Detail of *The Garden of Eden*

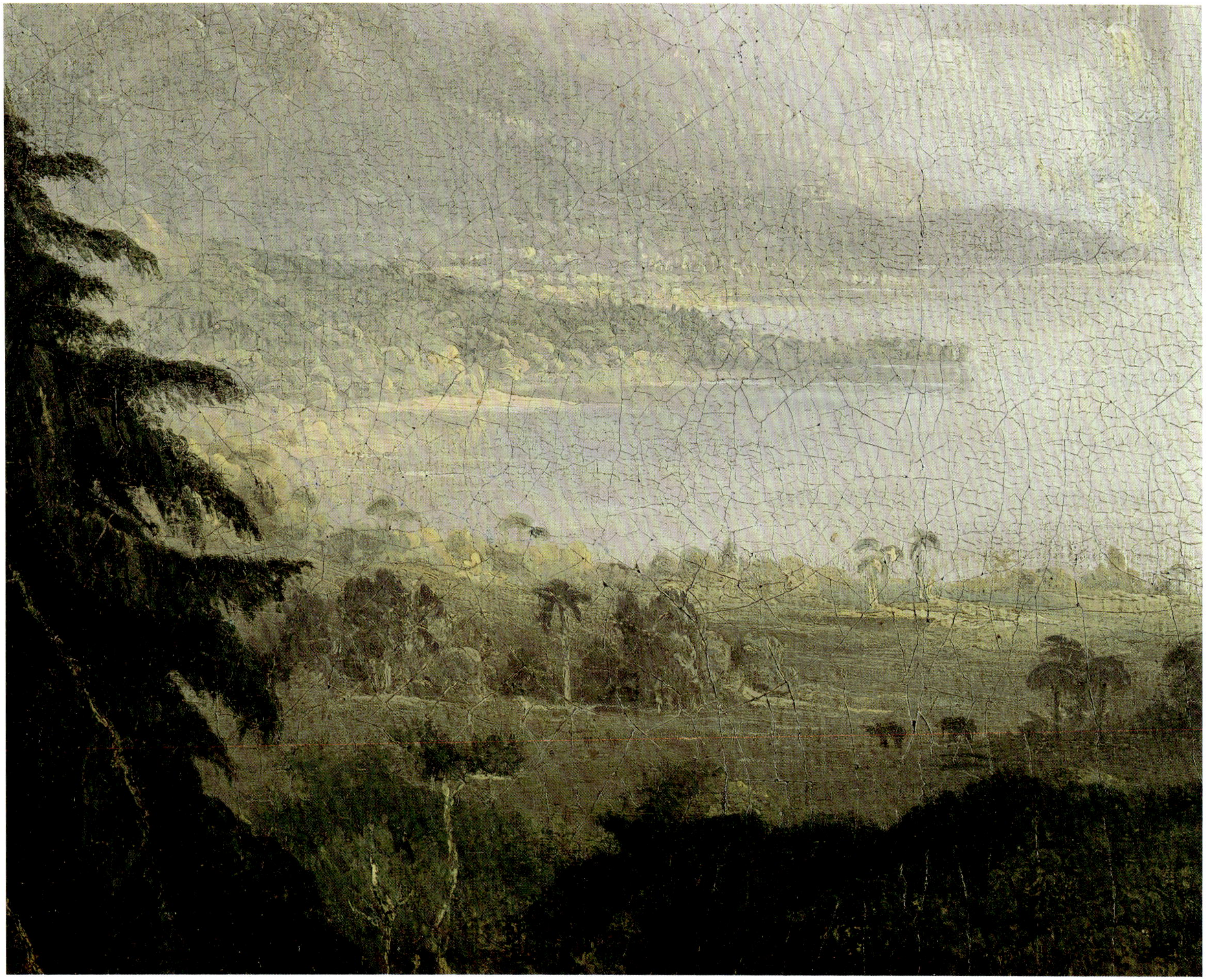

Plate 9. Detail of *The Garden of Eden*

"A Higher Style of Landscape": Thomas Cole's Paintings of Eden

IN MAY 1828 the landscape painter Thomas Cole wrote to one of his patrons with news of his latest efforts, which had just gone on view at the National Academy of Design in New York: "Amongst them are two attempts at a higher style of landscape than I have hitherto tried. The subject of one picture is The Garden of Eden. . . . The subject of the other is The Expulsion from the Garden."[1] Cole had eight paintings in the exhibition, but his words make it clear not only that he considered these two of particular importance but that he saw them as introducing a new phase in his art. He was right. *The Garden of Eden* (pl. 1), a lush and beautiful landscape filled with intricate detail, and *Expulsion from the Garden of Eden* (pl. 2), an intense and dramatic scene of cataclysmic natural forces, were the first full expressions of an extraordinarily fertile imagination. In these works landscape had indeed been elevated from mere description to something more richly meaningful. *The Garden of Eden* and *Expulsion from the Garden of Eden* were unlike anything Cole had done before, and they introduced a new approach to landscape painting that fundamentally changed the course of his career.

The importance of Cole's Eden paintings was not lost on his contemporaries. In virtually every major article or essay written about him in the years immediately following his death in 1848, they were singled out as watersheds precisely marking the moment when he moved from painting straightforward landscapes to something of a more profound order. For Cole, simply painting nature had become, according to the *North American Review*, "not enough. It was not merely an agreeable sensation that he asked from nature, but invigorating thought. . . . It was with this feeling . . . that he painted the 'Garden of Eden' and the 'Expulsion.'"[2] Creating the Eden pictures, said a reviewer for *Graham's Magazine* in 1855, "emptied a new current into the channel of his nature, that deepened the river of his thoughts."[3] And for the *Crayon* these paintings showed how Cole, "in the midst of a career from which few artists would have cared to deviate . . . determined to enter the higher sphere of imaginative composition."[4]

The Garden of Eden and *Expulsion from the Garden of Eden* have not, until the present exhibition, appeared together in public since 1829. *Expulsion* has maintained a prominent place in Cole's oeuvre, appearing in the 1848 memorial gathering of his works and in virtually every major exhibition devoted to him since. *The Garden of Eden*, however, dropped from sight and eventually became known to scholars of American art only through a small (and rather scarce) engraving after it (see fig. 36) and preparatory drawings (see figs. 14, 15).[5] None of these, of course, could give any indication of its color or confirm what Cole's contemporaries knew: "the Eden [was] a picture remarkable for its flowery luxuriance."[6] Its rediscovery in 1990 and subsequent purchase by the Amon Carter Museum were thus singularly fortuitous events, and returned to light what was unquestionably the most important missing piece in our knowledge of this key American artist. The story of the creation of Cole's paintings of Eden, of his intentions in them, and of the importance they held for his own art and that of others can at long last be more fully told.

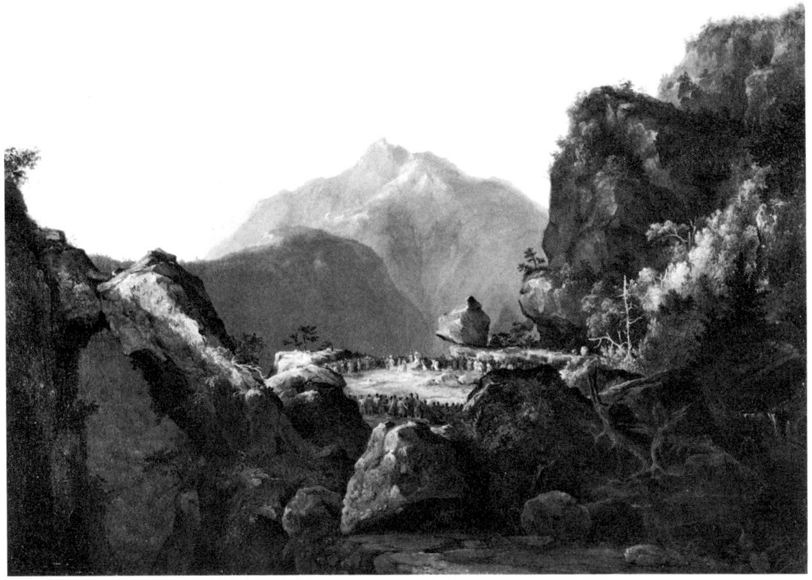

Figure 2. Thomas Cole, *Landscape Scene from "The Last of the Mohicans,"* oil on canvas, 1827, 25 x 31 in., New York State Historical Association, Cooperstown

Cole, encouraged by Gilmor's words, immediately replied: "I hope to profit by the excellent advice your letter contained, and shall show, in the pictures I have to paint for you, that I have not forgotten it."[14]

Cole lost no time in trying his hand at compositions and completed two such works by the time of the spring 1827 exhibition of the National Academy: *Landscape Composition, Saint John in the Wilderness* (Wadsworth Atheneum, Hartford) and *Landscape, Scene from "The Last of the Mohicans"* (Van Pelt Library, University of Pennsylvania, Philadelphia). In both, the scenery is rocky and mountainous, with huge cliffs and precipices dwarfing the tiny human figures. *Saint John in the Wilderness* and *Scene from "The Last of the Mohicans"* were generally well received, and both were soon sold, the former to Wadsworth and the latter to Dr. David Hosack of New York.[15] Cole's satisfaction with *"The Last of the Mohicans"* is evidenced by the fact that he subsequently created two more versions, one for Wadsworth (*Scene from "The Last of the Mohicans": Cora Kneeling at the Feet of Tamenund*, 1827, Wadsworth Atheneum, Hartford) and one for Gilmor (fig. 2), to satisfy his order for a third picture. In these new versions Cole drew inspiration from the dramatic scenery of New Hampshire's White Mountains, which he had toured (at Wadsworth's suggestion) during the summer of 1827. In particular, Cole had become greatly enamored of the distinctive features of Mount Chocorua (also called Corway, Corroway, or Carroway), which was the subject of the second landscape he painted for Gilmor (location unknown; fig. 3).[16] Gilmor, in spite of his doubts about Cole's readiness to attempt compositions, was generally pleased with his *Last of the Mohicans*, pronouncing it "most striking."[17] He did, however, fault it in one regard: "*Being a composition*, the arrangement of your rocks is artificial: the rock falling against another on the opposite side of a deep ravine, is finely rendered, but strikes the eye as something forced, & not ordinarily seen in nature. . . . The rock tottering on its pivot is scarcely *balanced* enough." But Cole had seen such things as natural bridges, erratic boulders, and rocking stones with his own eyes in the White Mountains (see figs. 22, 23), and by including these geological wonders he gave his landscape a scientifically correct but still highly dramatic charge.[18] As we shall see, the landscape in Gilmor's picture was but a prelude to the extraordinary geological panorama Cole would create in his *Expulsion*.

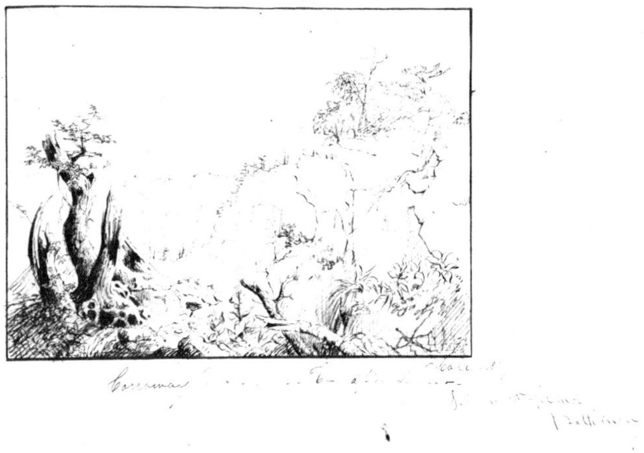

Figure 3. Thomas Cole, *Chocorua Peak*, pen and black ink over pencil, 1827, image: 6 1/16 x 8⅜ in., sheet: 9¼ x 15½ in., Detroit Institute of Arts

Cole's success with his first attempts at composed landscapes encouraged him to think of attempting something even more ambitious. Both the *Saint John* and the three versions of "*The Last of the Mohicans,*" even though compositions, were meant to be representations of places that actually existed. For his next effort Cole decided to paint a place that no human being (save two) had ever seen. He made up his mind to paint the Garden of Eden, a task that would require more imagination and skill than he had yet invested in a single picture.

Imagining the Garden of Eden

We do not know precisely when Cole first conceived of painting a picture of Eden, but the subject appears on a list that he began to keep in 1827 (fig. 4):

> Garden of Eden
>
> Distance – High mountains the highest with a cloud – Middle distance Lake one Island. Promontories with [sands?] – cliffs – nearer Plains with scattered trees – main water reflecting the [foremost?] Cascade – near undulating ground with trees – near the foreground a dark – deep recess with tall trees rising on the back side – a piece of still water – Foreground [with a rill?] pebbly bank – flowers – [Banana?] [lacy?] trees – the rill falling over a bit of white and varied marble – [Aside?] in the foreground [amongst?] the flowers [illegible] & something like a pedestal with the acanthus – Fruits, Flowers, Roses [daisies?], Violets, Hollyhocks, Poppies, M Glories, Sun Flower[s?] – Grapes, Oranges, Peaches, Melons, Apples, Bananas Animals. Antelopes, sheep – dog. Horse, Swans, Doves, Humming Bird[s?]. Bird of Paradise. Butterfly.[19]

The choppy style and inconsistent capitalization and punctuation of this description suggest that Cole was quickly jotting his thoughts down, quite possibly for the first time. And if this passage does represent his earliest thoughts about his planned painting, they were very well developed thoughts indeed, because the description comes close to the finished picture. On November 26, 1827, Cole wrote to Wadsworth to describe his plans for the picture, using similar but more fluid language:

> I am now painting in imagination a scene which I intend embodying on canvass for the next Exhibition – The subject is an extremely arduous one, and I am afraid that my strength in the Art will be but weakness in this attempt – The Garden of Eden is the subject – The scene as it exists in my minds eye, is very beautiful (as our own creations generally are) much more beautiful I know, than my art can realize; there is too much of Earth in paint and canvass – If I had time I should indulge myself in attempting to describe the scene I have imagined: but can now only say that there are in it lofty distant Mountains, a calm expansive lake, wooded bays, rocky promontories – a solitary island, undulating grounds, a meandering river, cascades, gentle lawns, groups of

Figure 4. Thomas Cole, Sketchbook page with list of subjects showing Garden of Eden entry, 1827, 7³⁄₁₆ x 9⅝ in., New York State Library, Albany, Manuscripts Division

> noble trees of various kinds, umbrageous recesses, a crystal rill with bed of brilliant marble, golden sands, pebbles of every dye – banks of beauteous flowers, fruits, harmless and graceful animals &c &c – I am sure I have fatigued you – but I must say that our first parents shall not be forgotten they are on the flowery threshold of their bower, watching the glorious sun, rise from his eastern couch – You will say if I paint all these things I shall have a full picture and it will take much time – It is so – the subject excites me and I must paint it even if I never sell the picture, which will most probably be the case – [20]

Surely one of the first places Cole must have turned as he contemplated painting his Eden would have been the relevant passages in the Book of Genesis (2:8–10):

> And the LORD God planted a garden eastward in E'den; and there he put the man whom he had formed. And out of the ground made the LORD God to grow every tree that is pleasant to the sight, and good for food; the tree of life also in the midst of the garden and the tree of knowledge of good and evil. And a river went out of E'den to water the garden; and from thence it was parted, and became into four heads.

Cole's language in his letter to Wadsworth (and, to a lesser extent, in his list of subjects) is much more descriptively rich than the biblical text, which suggests he may have consulted another source. In fact, as J. Bard McNulty has shown, he drew closely on John Milton's description of the Garden of Eden in lines 216–263 of Book 4 of *Paradise Lost*:[21]

> Out of this fertile ground he caused to grow
> All trees of noblest kind for sight, smell, taste;
> And all amid them stood the Tree of Life,
> High eminent, blooming ambrosial fruit
> Of vegetable gold; and next to Life
> Our death the Tree of Knowledge grew fast by,
> Knowledge of good bought dear by knowing ill.
> Southward through Eden went a river large,
> Nor changed his course, but through the shaggy hill
> Passed underneath ingulfed, for God had thrown
> That mountain as his garden mold high raised
> Upon the rapid current, which through veins
> Of porous earth with kindly thirst updrawn,
> Rose a fresh fountain, and with many a rill
> Watered the garden; thence united fell
> Down the steep glade, and met the nether flood,
> Which from his darksome passage now appears,
> And now divided into four main streams,
> Runs diverse, wandering many a famous realm
> And country whereof here needs no account,
> But rather to tell how, if art could tell,
> How from that sapphire fount the crispéd brooks,
> Rolling on orient pearl and sands of gold,
> With mazy error under pendant shades
> Ran nectar, visiting each plant, and fed
> Flow'rs worthy of Paradise which not nice art
> In beds and curious knots, but Nature boon

Figure 5. Antonio Molinari, *Adam and Eve*, oil on canvas, c. 1701–04, 47½ x 59 in., Ball State University Museum of Art, Muncie, Indiana, museum purchase with funds provided by the Joseph Johnson Charitable Trust and Richard and Dorothy Burkhardt

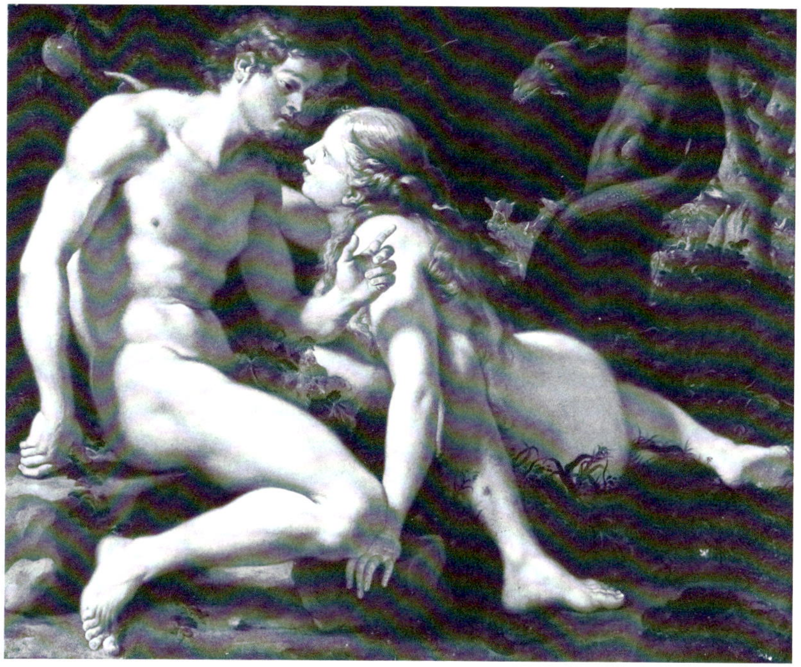

Poured forth profuse on hill and dale and plain,
Both where the morning sun first warmly smote
The open field, where th'unpierced shade
Imbrowned the noontide bow'rs: Thus was this place,
A happy rural seat of various view;
Groves whose rich trees wept odorous gums and balm,
Others whose fruit burnished with gold rind
Hung amiable, Hesperian fables true,
If true, here only, and of delicious taste.
Betwixt them lawns, or level downs, and flocks
Grazing the tender herb, were interposed,
Or palmy hillock, or the flow'ry lap
Of some irriguous valley spread her store,
Flowr's of all hue, and without thorn the rose.
Another side, umbrageous grots and caves
Of cool recess, o'er which the mantling vine
Lays forth her purple grape, and gently creeps
Luxuriant; meanwhile murmuring waters fall
Down the slope hills, dispersed, or in a lake,
That to the fringéd bank with myrtle crowned,
Her crystal mirror holds, unite their streams.

Given the fame of Milton's text, it is perfectly reasonable that Cole would have turned to it first for inspiration. But words, of course, are not pictures, and Cole's task now was to bring to life visually Milton's rich verbal imagery. As he began that task, presumably in December 1827, Cole may have first considered whether there were works by other artists that might offer guidance. The works of the still young American school would have been of little help, and Cole's exposure to original works by European painters at this point was limited to the few foreign pictures he could have seen in America. As he complained to Gilmor: "I have never yet seen a *fine picture* of any foreign painter."[22] Yet even though it may have been true that Cole had never seen a "*fine picture*," he most certainly had some knowledge of the great traditions of European landscape painting and such masters as Claude Lorrain and Salvator Rosa through books and prints. He had also seen at least a few European paintings at the Pennsylvania Academy of the Fine Arts while he was in Philadelphia in 1818 and again in 1824. Among the Academy's European paintings was a large *Adam and Eve* (fig. 5), which was then believed to be by the seventeenth-century artist Johann Carl Loth.[23] Perhaps Cole did recall this work as he began his own image of Eden, but it was a figure painting with Adam and Eve dominating the canvas and with very little of the Garden itself depicted. In fact, although there are many depictions of Adam and Eve in European painting from the late Middle Ages on, images focusing on the Garden are not as common. Perhaps the best-known examples

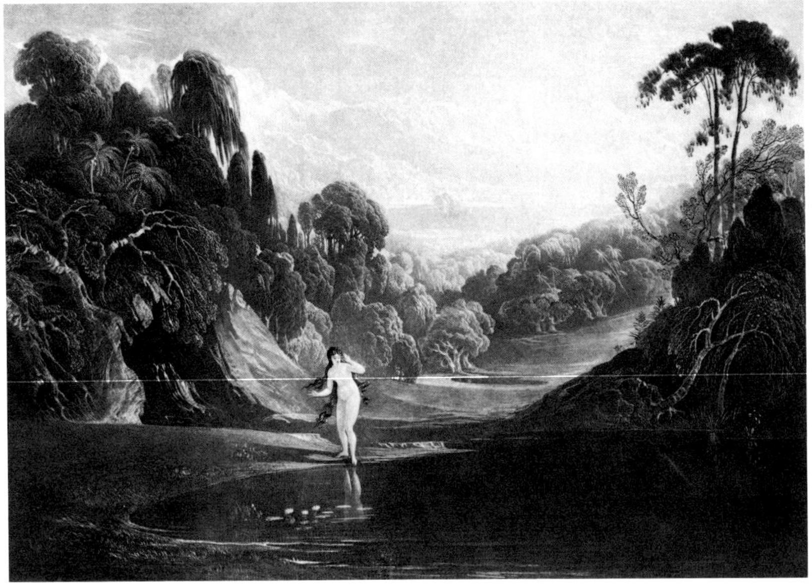

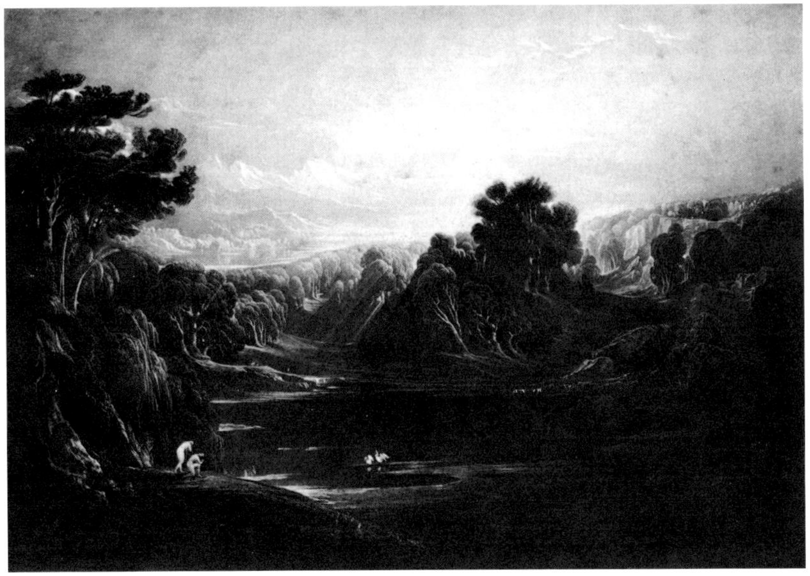

Figure 6 (*top*). John Martin, *Eve at the Fountain*, mezzotint proof from John Milton's *Paradise Lost*, 1827, plate: 10 x 13⅞ in., Museum of Fine Arts, Boston, gift of Samuel Glaser

Figure 7 (*bottom*). John Martin, *Adam and Eve – The Morning Hymn*, mezzotint in John Milton's *Paradise Lost*, 1827, image: 5¹¹⁄₁₆ x 8⅛ in., plate: 7¾ x 10¾ in., National Gallery of Art, Washington

are the "Paradise" paintings of the Flemish artist Jan Brueghel the Elder, who worked in the late sixteenth and early seventeenth centuries. Cole may have known of Brueghel's paintings of Eden from descriptions, but he almost certainly had not seen an actual example.[24]

However, Cole without doubt knew the works of the nineteenth-century English artist John Martin (1789–1854), who by the mid-1820s had created many images of the Garden of Eden. Martin, like Cole, was not an especially gifted figure painter and generally subordinated figures in his works to landscape and architectural elements. In most of his Eden images landscape predominates.[25] This is true of the twenty-four mezzotints illustrating Milton's *Paradise Lost*, which Martin created in 1823–25 and were published between 1825 and 1827.[26] For Cole, such works as Martin's *Eve at the Fountain* and *Adam and Eve – The Morning Hymn* (figs. 6, 7) would surely have helped in his own effort to imagine the Garden. Even though limited by the medium to black and white, Martin manipulated the mezzotint process to fill his images with wonderfully rich detail and subtle tonal contrasts. The *Eve*, like other illustrations for *Paradise Lost*, is notable for its profusion of trees of many types and shapes, ranging from deciduous to evergreens to palms. It is easy to imagine that Cole would have been greatly interested in such images, just as he was drawn to Milton's textual descriptions. Unfortunately, as we shall see, at least one of Cole's contemporaries would raise the issue of Martin's influence on the Eden paintings in a manner that was decidedly critical of the young painter.

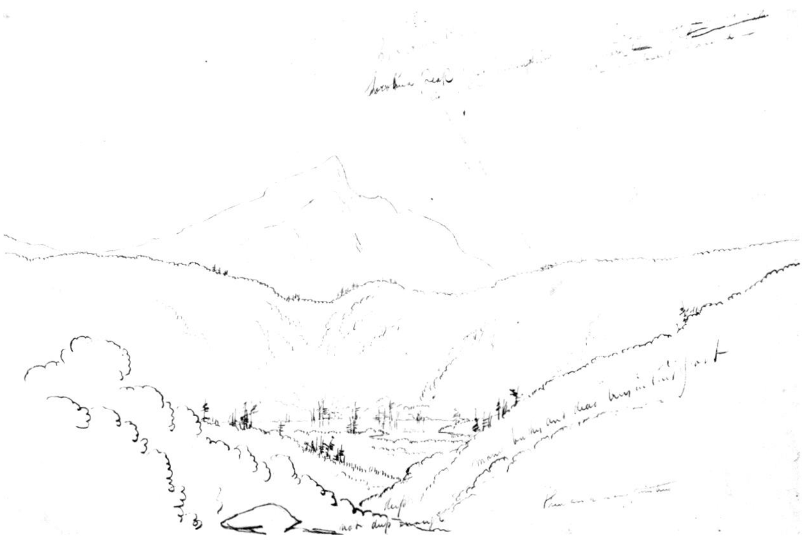

Figure 8. Thomas Cole, *Chocorua Peak, New Hampshire*, pen and black ink over pencil, c. 1827, 7⅞ x 12¼ in., Detroit Institute of Arts, Founders Society Purchase, William H. Murphy Fund

Painting The Garden of Eden

Our understanding of Cole's early methods of creating landscapes is, although perhaps not absolutely complete, relatively detailed, thanks to the large number of his sketches that have survived. We know from extant paintings and drawings and from references in his correspondence that his usual practice was to work from the studies he had created during his trips in the summer months in search of scenery. These were of two general types. On the one hand were panoramic landscape vistas that captured larger expanses of scenery (fig. 8); on the other were close-up studies of particular details of nature (trees, branches, rocks, flowers, etc.) of the kind that Cole had done since the earliest days of his career. Without question, Cole exercised a certain amount of creative freedom in using material from his drawings. Even when portraying actual scenes (as in *Sunrise in the Catskills*, see fig. 1), he often included elements in the foreground such as blasted trees that may have been seen and sketched elsewhere. In that regard, his early works were already, at least according to Gilmor's standards, tending toward composed landscapes. That, in part, explains why he was so quick in his correspondence with the Baltimore patron to explain why he thought composed landscapes could still be considered successful. As he observed: "the most lovely and perfect parts of Nature may be brought together, and combined in a whole that shall surpass in beauty and effect any picture painted from a single view."[27] Moreover, Cole, in justifying his interest in compositions, provided a concise explanation of his own methods: "He who would paint compositions, and not be false, must sit down amidst his sketches, make selections, combine them, and so have nature for every object he paints."[28]

If Cole followed his own words to the letter, he must have sat down amidst his sketches as he began to paint *The Garden of Eden* and looked for ones that could help him. Among his most recent panoramic drawings were several from his previous summer's visit to the White Mountains. As we have seen, Cole was particularly attracted by the features of Mount Chocorua, and in several drawings (for example, fig. 8) the mountain dominates the distance, with lower hills and a lake appearing in the middle ground. What this drawing depicts, in fact, seems remarkably like the background Cole imagined in his earliest description of *The Garden of Eden*, with its "high mountain" [and] "Middle distance Lake." Having already made use of Chocorua-inspired scenery in the Wadsworth and Gilmor "*Last of the Mohicans*," Cole did not hesitate to adapt the mountain once again, although for *The Garden of Eden* he would reverse its profile and make its contours even more precipitous.[29]

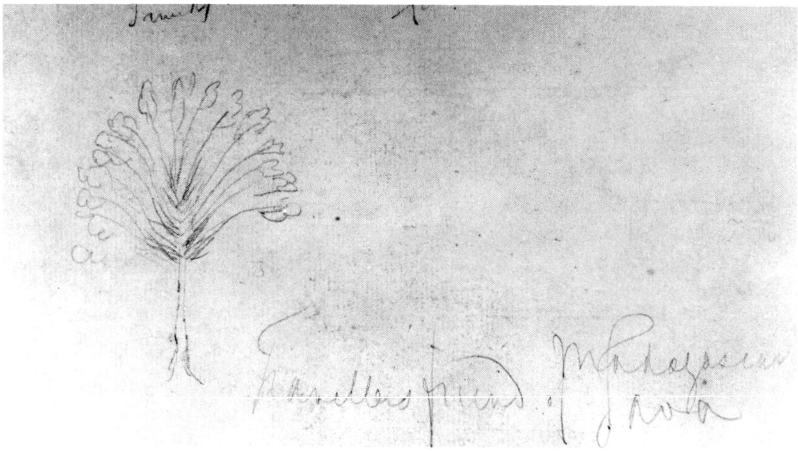

Figure 9. Thomas Cole, Detail of sketchbook page with travellers' palm, graphite on paper, 1827/28, 9 5/8 x 7 3/16 in., New York State Library, Albany, Manuscripts Division

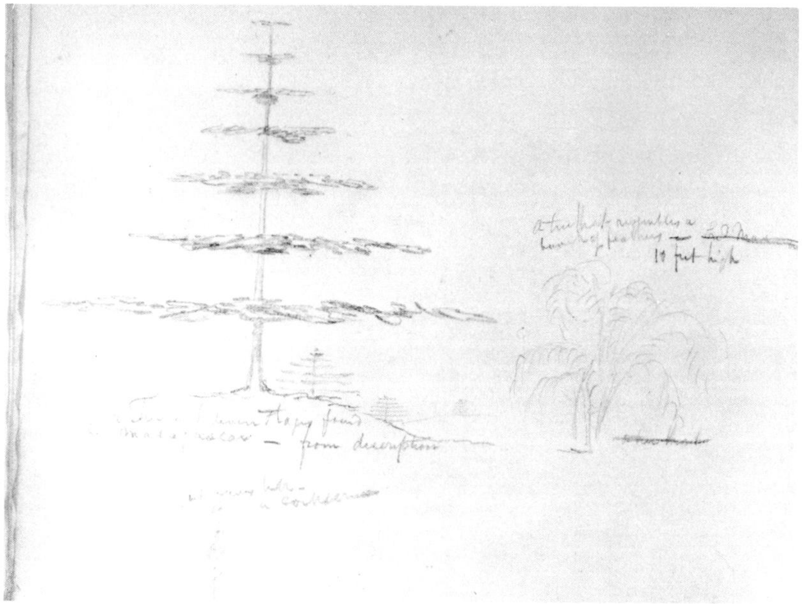

Figure 10. Thomas Cole, Detail of sketchbook page with Madagascar trees, graphite on paper, 1827/28, 9 5/8 x 7 3/16 in., New York State Library, Albany, Manuscripts Division

However, the foreground of his painting, with its myriad exotic trees, plants, flowers, and animals, would obviously be unlike any particular place Cole had sketched in America. To be sure, he could study specific flowers and plants available to him in the northeastern United States, and there are a number of surviving sketches to indicate that he did. Among the flowers identifiable in the foreground of the painting are hollyhocks, roses, strawberry plants, lilies, iris, narcissus, hyacinths, false-dragon head, delphiniums, and tulips, all of which Cole could have seen in gardens and hothouses in northeastern America. But he may have had to turn elsewhere for some of the more exotic species. One place Cole could turn was his own memory, for he had made a trip to the island of Saint Eustatia (Eustatius) in the West Indies in 1819.[30] No sketches survive from that trip, and it is unclear whether Cole even made any while there.[31] Fortunately, however, he did leave us a written record of the island's scenery in a short story called "Emma Moreton, a West Indian Tale," which was published in 1825. One passage in particular suggests that Cole's brief visit to the West Indies left him with memories that might have played a role in the creation of *The Garden of Eden*:

> The highest mountain of St. Eustatia is intersected on its southern side by a narrow valley or ravine, down whose channel the roaring torrent sweeps in the hurricane and rainy months, but which was now blooming in all the richness and luxuriance of a tropical soil. Here the deep green orange blossoms and bears – here the bright banana hangs its ample and silky leaves, which, as they chafe each other in the breeze, yield a sweet and whispering music; and an hundred shrubs and plants, known only to these sunny climes, flourish in their native elegance and beauty.[32]

Figure 11. Thomas Cole, Sketchbook page with exotic bird and color notes, 1827/28, 6½ x 4 in., Detroit Institute of Arts, Founders Society Purchase, William H. Murphy Fund

Cole's words make it clear that this lovely landscape was as close as he had ever come to seeing something that approximated his imagined vision of Eden. As one contemporary source observed: "Cole was charmed with St. Eustatia. . . . Everything was tropical and of an exuberant richness."[33]

However, Cole apparently felt he needed to give his landscape an even greater sense of the exotic, for he placed a plant called a traveller's palm prominently in the middle distance. This distinctive and unusual tree is native to one region of the island of Madagascar in the Indian Ocean but was widely cultivated in botanical gardens by the nineteenth century. Also known as the traveller's tree, traveller's friend, and raven palm (*Ravenala madagascariensis*), the plant is notable for the distinctive fan-shaped arrangement of its leaves. Its common names reflect the fact that its leaves gather and store rainwater, which supposedly could be tapped by a thirsty traveler. Cole's painted version of it, although not correct in every detail, is sufficiently accurate to suggest that he had seen an example and drawn it from life (fig. 9). One likely place he could have sketched a traveller's palm was in New York's Elgin Gardens, which were founded in 1801.[34] He had, however, apparently also read about such things, for in his sketchbooks there are several drawings of trees (fig. 10) with the notation "Madagascar." One of these, inscribed "a tree with seven stages found in Madagascar," also includes the phrase "from description," suggesting that Cole based that drawing on a text. And though we do not know for certain what that text was, it was presumably something like *A History of the Island of Madagascar* (1822), by Samuel Copland, which includes detailed descriptions of the trees found on the island.[35] Many exotic and faraway lands were becoming known to nineteenth-century readers through such history and travel books, and certainly Madagascar, with its remarkably diverse flora, might well have struck many people as Edenic.

Cole may have made many other detailed studies for specific elements in *The Garden of Eden*, but only a few other extant drawings may be reasonably associated with it. One is a sheet with two drawings of a long-tailed exotic bird, with the colors of the plumage carefully noted (fig. 11), which was surely the source for the bird perched just below the figures of Adam and Eve. The other (fig. 12) shows a grove of trees very similar to that bordering the stream in the middle distance at the far left of the painting. This drawing is inscribed "Memorandum from Pillement."[36] "Pillement" was presumably

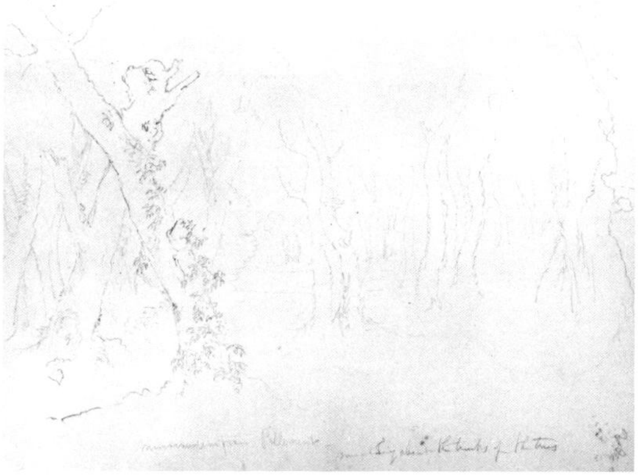

Figure 12. Thomas Cole, Sketchbook page inscribed "Memorandum from Pillement," graphite on paper, 1827/28, 7³⁄₁₆ x 9⅝ in., New York State Library, Albany, Manuscripts Division

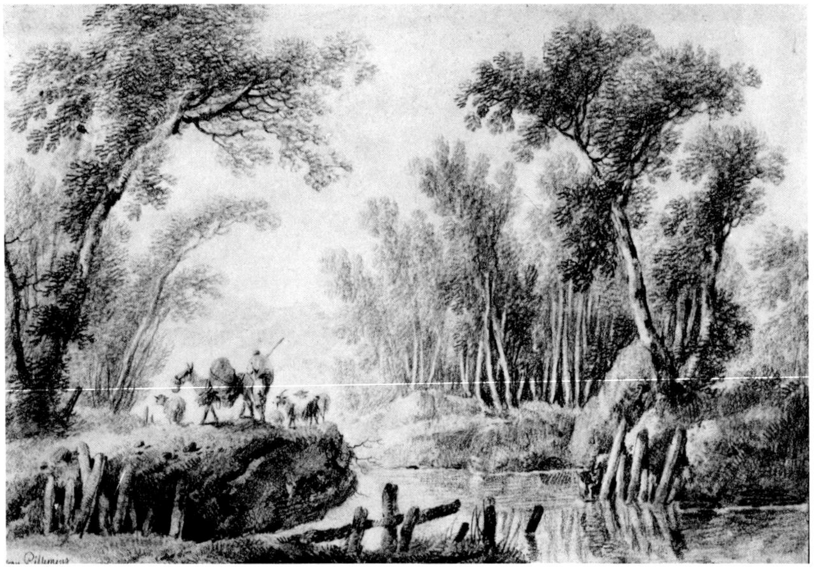

Figure 13. Jean Pillement, *Man with Mule, Goats by a Stream*, pencil, 1792, 16 x 21¼ in., Philadelphia Museum of Art

the Frenchman Jean-Baptiste Pillement (1728–1808), a creator of landscapes and decorative images who was particularly well known for his chinoiserie prints.[37] Similar groves of trees appear in many of Pillement's landscapes (fig. 13), but whether Cole saw an actual work by him, or merely a print after one of his works, is simply not known.[38]

Of course, no matter how carefully Cole may have pondered specific details as he planned his *Garden of Eden*, the major task he faced was to conceive its overall composition. That apparently was done in two steps, each documented by a careful drawing. In the first of these (fig. 14) Cole worked out the basic concept of a flower-filled foreground, middle-distance meadows surrounded by large trees, and pyramidal mountain terminating the view. An inscription reading "the fringe of trees going perspectively off" suggests that Cole intended from the first to use the receding ranks of trees to help establish a sense of vast space. The second, more finished drawing (fig. 15) is quite close to the painting, lacking only the figures of Adam and Eve, the various birds and animals, and the dark cave above the lake at the right. Inscribed at the top "Garden of Eden," this drawing also includes a crescent moon at the upper left corner; a similar moon originally appeared slightly lower in the painting but has now become almost completely transparent as the pigments have aged.

In a letter of March 11, 1828, to Daniel Wadsworth, Cole indicated that he had devoted considerable time to creating the painting:

> I have been closely confined all Winter – occupied principally in my large picture of the Garden of Eden – the Labour I have bestowed on it is great – and I hope not without effect – for the last

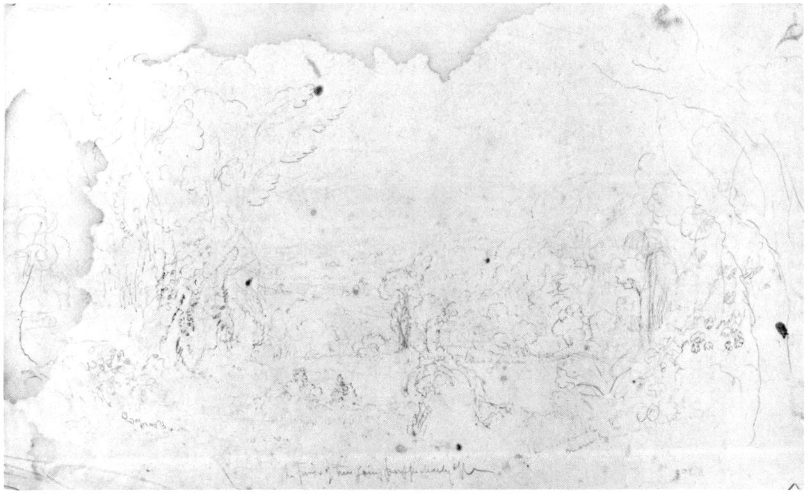

Figure 14. Thomas Cole, Study for *The Garden of Eden*, pencil, 1827/28, 7½ x 12¾ in., Detroit Institute of Arts, Founders Society Purchase, William H. Murphy Fund

Figure 15. Thomas Cole, Study for *The Garden of Eden*, pen and black ink over pencil, 1827/28, 10 x 15⅚16 in., Detroit Institute of Arts, Founders Society Purchase, William H. Murphy Fund

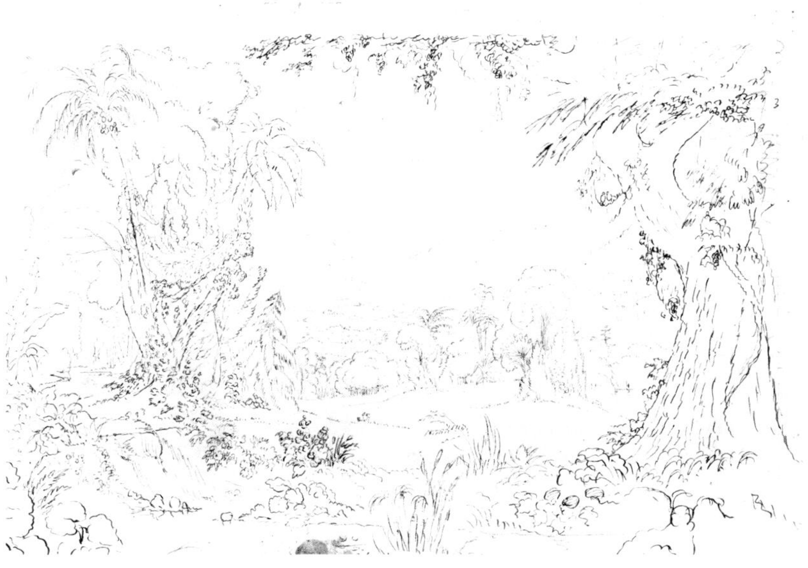

> week so many parties have called to see it that I scarcely work at all – I have now concluded not to shew it to any till the Exhibition opens – I have found it necessary to do so – Notwithstanding it *appears* attractive (perhaps a whim of fashion). I know it to have a multitude of faults and a great want of beauties.[39]

Those fortunate enough to have an advance look at Cole's new painting must have been dazzled by what they saw. Cole had filled a canvas measuring three by four-and-a-half feet with an astounding variety of plant and animal forms, creating an image that seems both connected in some way to the real world of experience and yet also part of a world of pure fantasy. We see things that remind us of the world we know and inhabit – flowers, leaves, great trees, birds, a squirrel, a pair of swans gliding on the river, meadows, deer, a lake, mountains – but they add up to a world that we rationally know cannot exist. Where on earth could there be a place where lush tropical palms and plants grow side by side with those from colder climates, where streams could be filled with enormous gemstones of many colors? Where, in short, could there be such a paradise? Cole, in a startlingly vivid and wonderfully detailed way, had managed – on canvas at least – to bring the Garden of Eden back into existence.

Painting a Companion: Expulsion from the Garden of Eden

So far as we know, Cole's original plan was to paint just one picture of Eden. There was no mention of a companion piece in his first entry about Eden on his list of subjects (see fig. 4). However, six entries later there appears (fig. 16): "Expulsion of Adam & Eve from the Garden of Eden – with stupendous mountain walls."[40] Cole also did not initially mention such a work in his correspondence with Wadsworth, but in April he

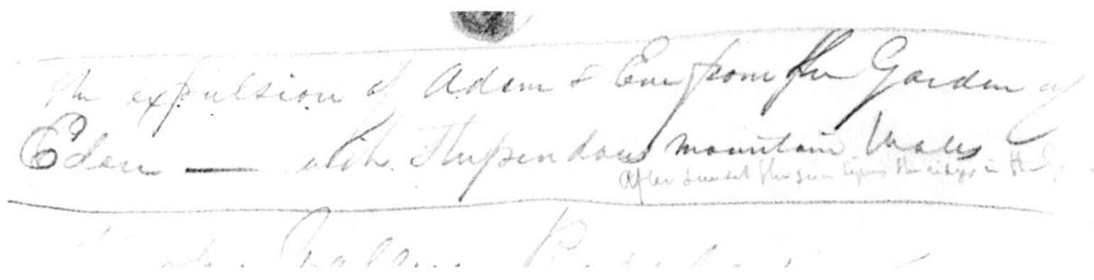

Figure 16. Thomas Cole, Detail of sketchbook page with list of subjects showing first *Expulsion* entry, graphite on paper, 1827/28, 9⅝ x 7³⁄16 in., New York State Library, Albany, Manuscripts Division

announced: "I am endeavouring to finish for Exhibition a companion picture to the Garden of Eden – 'The Expulsion of our first Parents from Eden.'"[41] As we know, Cole did manage to finish this new picture in time for the opening of the National Academy of Design's third annual exhibition in early May, so he must have painted it with considerable speed. However, as was the case with *The Garden of Eden*, *Expulsion* greatly taxed Cole's creative abilities. Indeed, even though it occurred over a shorter span of time, its evolution was highly complex. We may only speculate as to why Cole took on this additional

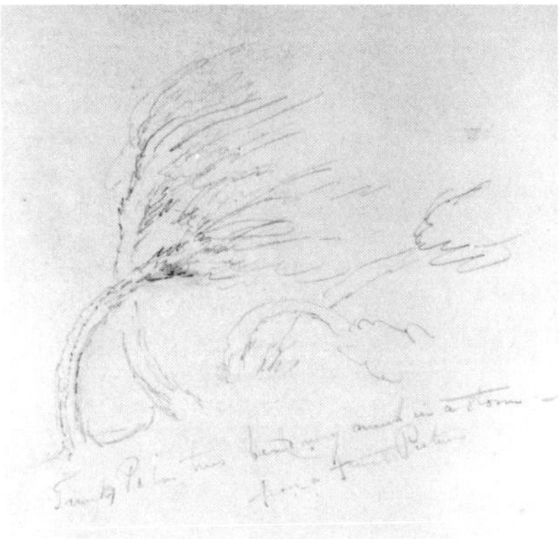

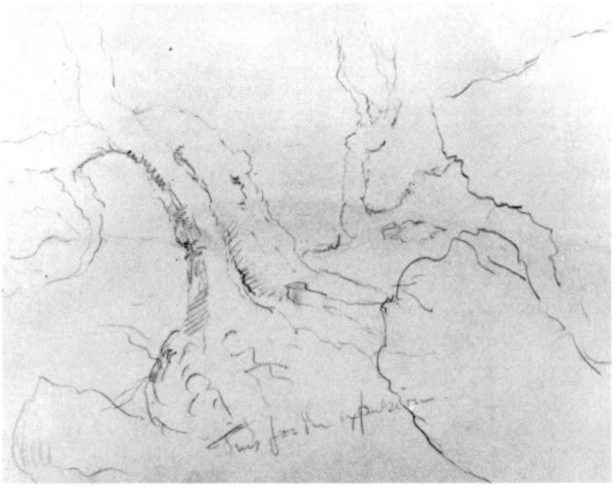

Figure 17 (*top*). Thomas Cole, Detail of sketchbook page with trees for the *Expulsion*, graphite on paper, probably 1828, 9⅝ x 7³⁄₁₆ in., New York State Library, Albany, Manuscripts Division

Figure 18 (*bottom*). Thomas Cole, Sketchbook page with trees for the *Expulsion*, graphite on paper, probably 1828, 7³⁄₁₆ x 9⅝ in., New York State Library, Albany, Manuscripts Division

burden, but perhaps it was because he felt the need for narrative closure. By this time the final prints in Martin's *Paradise Lost* series had appeared, the last of which was, in fact, *Adam and Eve Driven out of Paradise* (see fig. 34).[42]

There are many drawings related to *Expulsion from the Garden of Eden*, and although several are of details of trees (figs. 17–19), most relate to the overall composition. This suggests that Cole's major challenge lay in the general conception of the *Expulsion*, which was more grandly dramatic but less intricately detailed than its pendant. Meeting that challenge resulted in some of Cole's most exceptional drawings (see figs. 26–29, 30–32) and a striking unfinished canvas (pl. 3).

There are more than a half-dozen compositional drawings in the *Expulsion* series, and several more that are related to it. And even though there is no firm evidence telling us the exact order of these works, a reasonable sequence of events can be postulated.[43] A verbal indication of Cole's thinking appears on the same sketchbook page (fig. 20) where the artist made his drawings of trees from Madagascar: "Expulsion from the garden – Distant mountains dark on cloudy volcano – black torrent – Gulf – Trees bending before the storm – Dead trees – Trees with contorted branches/Vulture Hyena Tiger[s?] – Birds of Prey of several kinds – Thorns – Rain – Eagle – Snakes – Feather tree." These words are so similar to the final painting that one wonders whether they were written not at the beginning of the creative process, but late in it. Certainly the drawing on the page immediately following (fig. 21) does not bear much resemblance to the final image, for it shows the positions of the Garden and the outside world reversed (the former on the left, the latter on the right) and has a figure (presumably the angel with the flaming sword) perched on a rocky pinnacle, with the tiny figures of Adam and Eve at the lower right. Still, this drawing includes the notations "clouds in a whirlwind" and "rain," which do hint at the meteorological drama of the final painting. There is also another verbal indication of Cole's thinking: "Expulsion from the Garden of Eden The wall of the Garden running [?] through the picture with the Expulsion [illegible] on the left the Garden of Eden in all its beauty on the right the world in its deformity rugged dark stormy Broken Rocks – Rugged trees – ."

However, at some point early in his studies for the *Expulsion*, Cole apparently abandoned this two-part landscape scheme contrasting the world and the Garden and began working with a more centrally focused composition depicting a natural rock bridge. This motif was derived from something Cole had seen on his 1827 visit to the White Mountains – a natural arch formed by what he called an "overhanging rock" (fig. 22).[44] This became the basis of several other sketches showing two projecting rocks with a huge boulder wedged between them. Cole inscribed one of these drawings "The Bridge of Fear" (fig. 23), a title that also appears on his list of possible

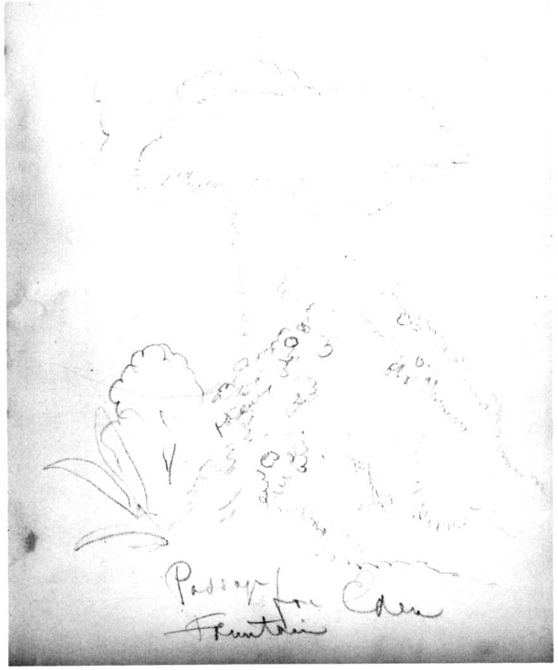

Figure 19. Thomas Cole, Sketchbook page inscribed "Passage for Eden Fountain," graphite on paper, probably 1828, 9⅝ x 7³⁄₁₆ in., New York State Library, Albany, Manuscripts Division

Figure 20. Thomas Cole, Detail of sketchbook page with Madagascar trees and *Expulsion* description, graphite on paper, 1827/28, 9⅝ x 7³⁄₁₆ in., New York State Library, Albany, Manuscripts Division

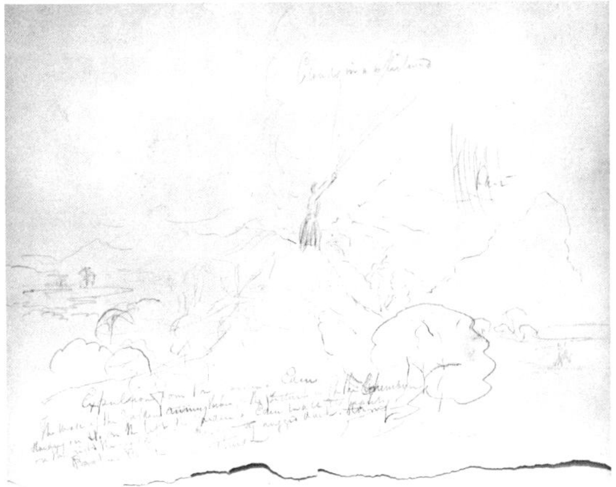

Figure 21. Sketchbook page with study for the *Expulsion*, graphite on paper, probably 1828, 7³⁄₁₆ x 9⅝ in., New York State Library, Albany, Manuscripts Division

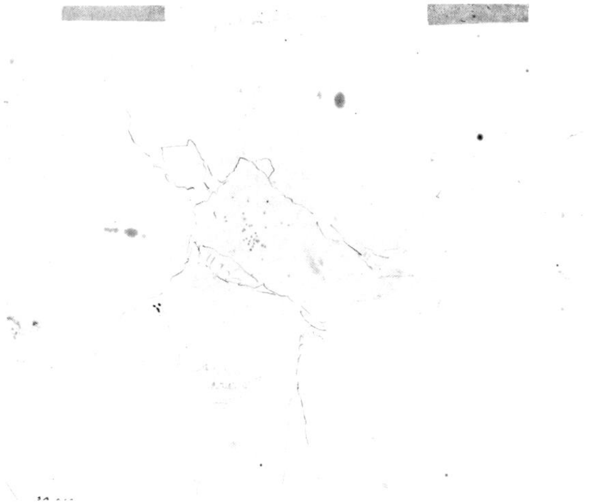

Figure 22. Thomas Cole, *Overhanging Rock*, pencil, 1827, 7⅞ x 9⁷⁄₁₆ in., Detroit Institute of Arts, Founders Society Purchase, William H. Murphy Fund

Figure 23. Thomas Cole, *The Bridge of Fear*, pencil, 1827, 7⅞ x 9⁷⁄₁₆ in., Detroit Institute of Arts, Founders Society Purchase, William H. Murphy Fund

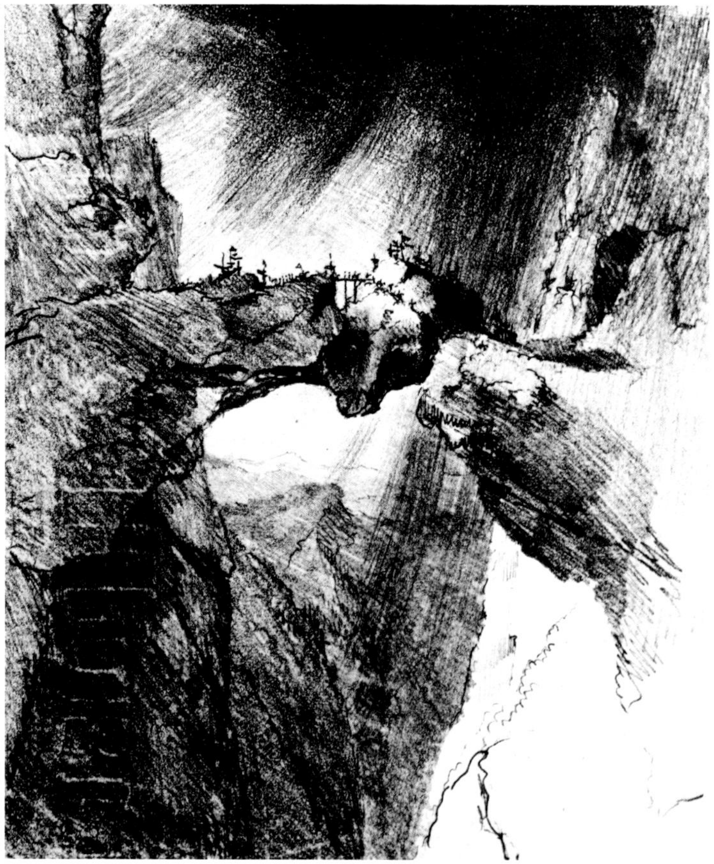

Figure 24. Thomas Cole, *The Bridge of Fear*, pencil, 1827/28, image: 5¾ x 4⅞ in., sheet: 9¼ x 7½ in., Detroit Institute of Arts, Founders Society Purchase, William H. Murphy Fund

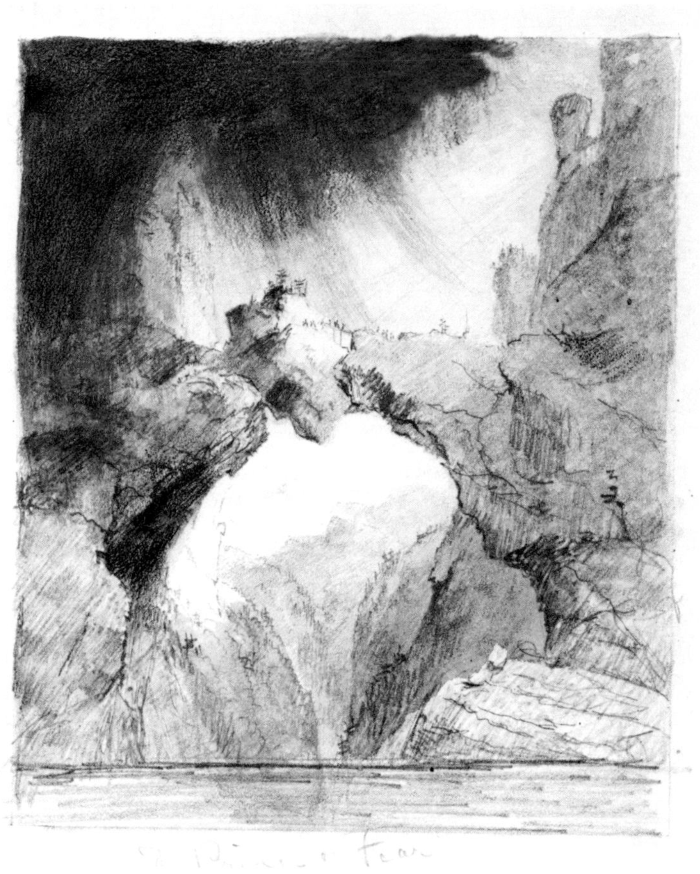

Figure 25. Thomas Cole, *The Bridge of Fear*, graphite and black crayon with gray wash, 1827/28, 9 9/16 x 7 3/16 in., National Gallery of Art, Washington, John Davis Hatch Collection

subjects. Cole also made at least two highly finished and dramatic drawings (figs. 24, 25) of the formation, incorporating a rain-swept sky above. These drawings, and the inclusion of "The Bridge of Fear" on the list of subjects, suggest Cole was considering executing a painting of this subject, but there is no evidence that he ever did.

Instead, the "bridge-of-fear" motif became the basis for a group of drawings (figs. 26–29) that may well represent Cole's revised thinking for the composition of the *Expulsion* after he abandoned the initial two-part scheme (see fig. 21). The first was possibly the one most like the "bridge-of-fear" drawings (fig. 26). Like those, it shows the rock formation as arched in

Figure 26 (*top*). Thomas Cole, Sketchbook page with "Bridge of Fear/Expulsion" #1, graphite on paper, 1828, 7 3/16 x 9 5/8 in., New York State Library, Albany, Manuscripts Division

Figure 27 (*bottom*). Thomas Cole, Sketchbook page with "Bridge of Fear/Expulsion" #2, graphite on paper, 1828, 7 3/16 x 9 5/8 in., New York State Library, Albany, Manuscripts Division

form, with a large boulder wedged in the middle; our vantage point is from slightly below, and we can see through the arch a landscape far in the distance. The major differences between this drawing and the "bridge-of-fear" group are that a large, freestanding rock arch with raylike lines emanating from it has replaced the mountainside at the right, and two tiny figures are now visible on the bridge itself. A very similar drawing (fig. 27), with the bridge now less arched but still with a view of a distant landscape under it, is inscribed at the bottom "Expulsion." In the third drawing (fig. 28), however, Cole transformed the motif considerably. Our vantage point is now more distant and slightly higher, so that we are almost level with the bridge, rather than looking up at it. The bridge itself now has virtually no arch, and we no longer see under it toward a distant scene. Instead, higher mountains – one of which is clearly volcanic – terminate the view; a few lines running vertically through the center of the sheet suggest a waterfall. Though only a hastily executed sketch, this drawing is nevertheless remarkably suggestive of Cole's creative process and vividly shows how far his imagination had taken him from his original inspiration in the "overhanging rock in the White Mountains."

The fourth drawing in this series (fig. 29) is similar in composition to the one just discussed but includes an inscription at the bottom reading "Scale of Colour for the Expulsion." In it a series of concentric circles, each inscribed with a color, radiate from the rock arch. Reading from the innermost circle out, the colors are yellow, orange, red, purple, mauve [blue?]; there is also an inscription reading "blue" in the upper right, and a wedge-shaped area at the lower left inscribed "green."[45] Al-

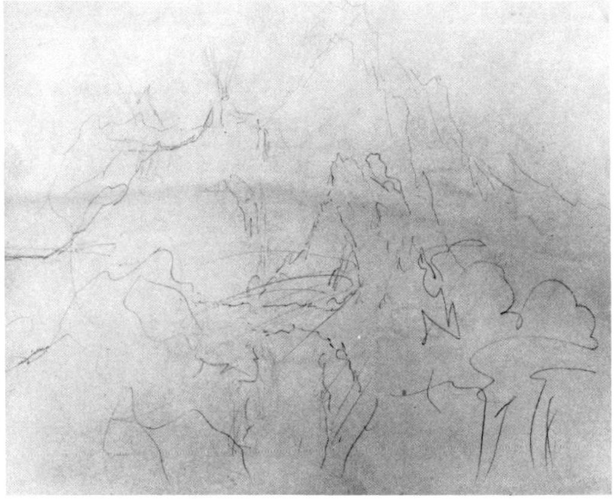

Figure 28. Thomas Cole, Sketchbook page with "Bridge of Fear/Expulsion" #3, graphite on paper, 1828, 7 3/16 x 9 5/8 in., New York State Library, Albany, Manuscripts Division

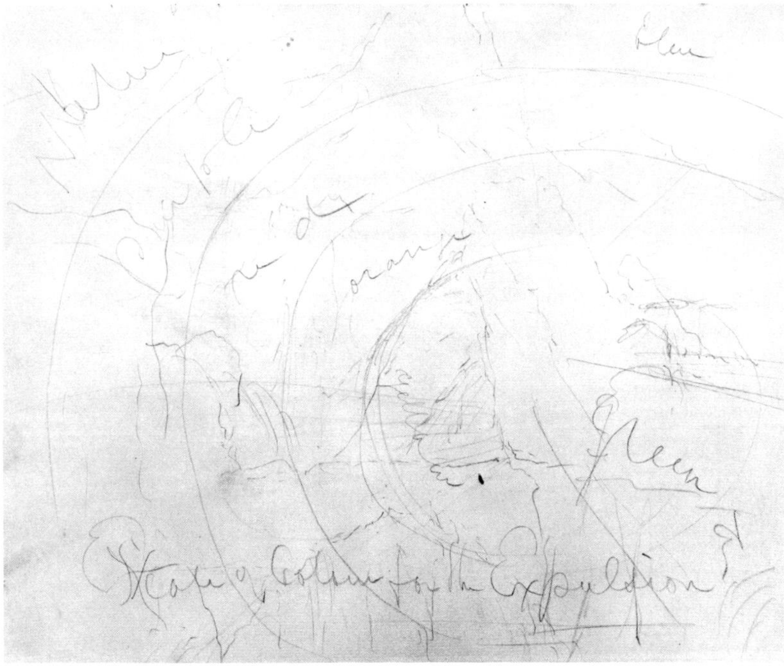

Figure 29. Thomas Cole, Sketchbook page inscribed "Scale of Colour for Expulsion," graphite on paper, 1828, 7 3/16 x 9 5/8 in., New York State Library, Albany, Manuscripts Division

though the correspondence is not exact, this arrangement does relate closely to the color scheme of the unfinished canvas now known as *Expulsion – Moon and Firelight* (pl. 3), with its glimpse of the green fields and blue skies of Eden at the right, yellow fire in the arch, orange-lit bridge, volcano spewing red lava, and dark sky at the upper left.[46]

None of the "bridge-of-fear" drawings for the *Expulsion* shows much of the Garden of Eden itself. Presumably Cole initially saw no reason to include it, for its appearance could be amply represented by his first picture. Thus, in the Thyssen painting (pl. 3), which is very similar to the third and fourth drawings discussed above, the Garden is only vaguely suggested at the far right; Cole's attention at this point was still firmly fixed on the dramatic rocky landscape of the world outside. However, as the unfinished state of this picture indicates, Cole put it aside, apparently unsatisfied with what was admittedly a most dramatic beginning.[47]

We do not know for certain what Cole's next step was, but it seems that he returned to working with the idea of a two-part composition showing both the Garden and the outside world. Three drawings in the Detroit Institute of Arts (figs. 30–32) show the evolution of the new scheme. In what was probably the first (fig. 30), Cole pulled back the vantage point and expanded the composition from what it had been in the "bridge-of-fear" series to create three distinct zones of space. On the right, quickly sketched tall palm trees frame a view showing much more of the Garden of Eden. At the center, large rocks mark the portal at the edge of Eden, and sweeping lines at the left side suggest a rainstorm. In what appears to be

Figure 30. Thomas Cole, Study for *Expulsion from the Garden of Eden*, pencil, 1828, 9¹³⁄₁₆ x 15⅝ in., Detroit Institute of Arts, Founders Society Purchase, William H. Murphy Fund

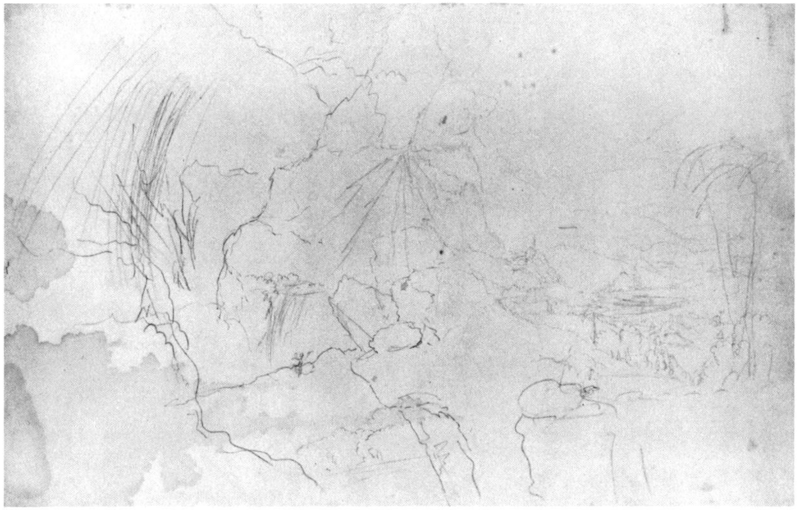

the next in the series (fig. 31), Cole more carefully drew in the forms of Eden and traced the outlines of the massive rocks and added several new elements, including diminutive figures of Adam and Eve, a volcano puffing smoke in the distance, and windblown trees very much like those he had noted in his sketchbook (see figs. 17, 18). The third drawing (fig. 32) is closely related to the preceding one but is even more finished and detailed, with ink washes creating a strong contrast between light and dark areas. Justly considered one of Cole's most dramatically effective drawings, this sheet has all the hallmarks of a carefully considered final study.

When we turn to the finished picture (see pl. 2), we see that it is similar to this last drawing in both detail and effect. However, we also see that Cole reintroduced the motif of the natural bridge, a feature he had left out of the drawings (or perhaps had treated so sketchily as to make reading its form difficult). Thus, in the end, Cole drew on aspects he had investigated in all of his preliminary studies. He also encircled the erupting volcano in a vortex of rain and clouds that is somewhat reminiscent of the two finished "bridge-of-fear" drawings (see figs. 24, 25). Finally, Cole added a dramatic tableau at the lower left, with a hyenalike animal poised over a dead stag and a vulture flying close by. The result was a work of exceptional force and power, with compositional energies that seem ready to burst from the canvas in all directions. In what is surely one of the most dramatic oppositions in all of landscape painting, the calm and serene order of the Garden is juxtaposed with a dark and troubled world, where nature's forces seem to have run unpredictably wild.[48]

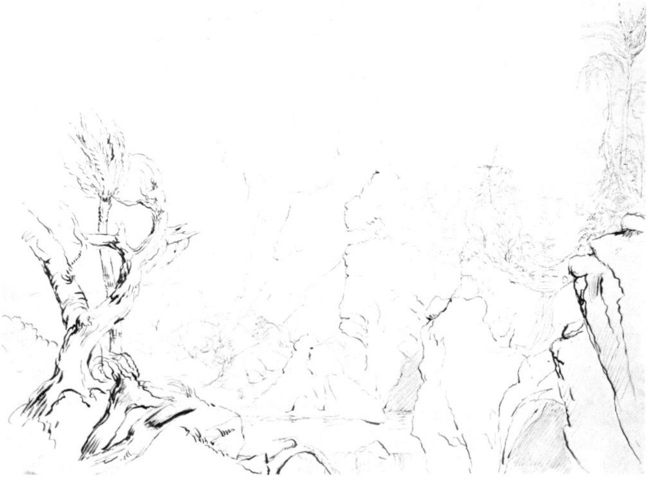

Figure 31. Thomas Cole, Study for *Expulsion from the Garden of Eden*, pen and black ink, wash, and pencil, 1828, 13¹³⁄₁₆ x 19⁵⁄₁₆ in., Detroit Institute of Arts, Founders Society Purchase, William H. Murphy Fund

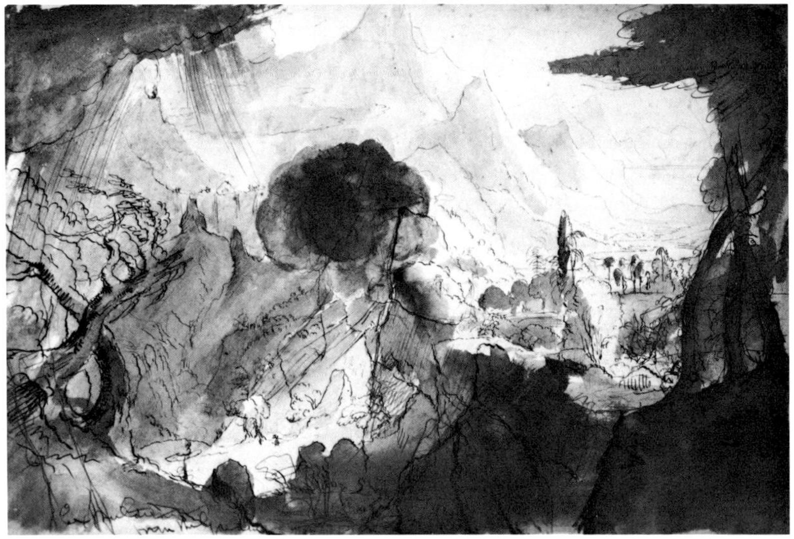

Figure 32. Thomas Cole, Study for *Expulsion from the Garden of Eden*, pen, pencil, and wash, 1828, 11 x 16½ in., Detroit Institute of Arts, Founders Society Purchase, William H. Murphy Fund

The Garden of Eden *and* Expulsion from the Garden of Eden *Exhibited*

In his letter to Daniel Wadsworth of March 11, 1828, Cole said his intention was to exhibit *The Garden of Eden*, which was then nearing completion, in the next exhibition of the National Academy of Design. That was doubtless his plan from the first, for the academy offered unquestionably the most prestigious setting for debuting an important work. The Hartford patron, who made a visit to New York in April and examined both pictures, later wrote to Cole and critiqued them.[49] His letter is unfortunately lost, but Cole's reply survives:

> I am much obliged to you for having thoughts of my pictures after you left me – but I cannot entirely agree with you in thinking the cave (or Grotto) formal; indeed I do not well know how that term can be applied to such an object – It may have something of gloom about it and that was my intention in painting it – Though a cave may be a gloomy object in Nature – a *view* of its entrance gives rise to those trains of pensive feeling and thought that I have always found the most exquisitely delightful – The poets often speak of caves, and grottos as pleasing objects, and I do not know why the painter may not think as a poet – it is a cool retreat during the Noon-day heats – I should have considered my picture imperfect without it – as wanting one of the *fine features* of Nature all of which are beautiful in their places – Had I more time, and was not afraid of fatiguing you I would enter into the reasons for what I have done more particularly – for it is always my intention to introduce nothing in a picture for which I cannot give a good reason.[50]

Cole's rather defensive reaction to Wadsworth's critique is understandable when we recall that he was extremely anxious about how his paintings would be received once they went on public display. That test came in early May at the National Academy,[51] and Cole no doubt waited anxiously for the first reviews.

The initial response was generally positive. The reviewer for the *New-York Mirror* considered the Eden pictures "the most prominent" of the eight works by Cole in the exhibition and wrote of *The Garden of Eden*:

> [It] is a composition exhibiting a rich and luxurious assemblage of natural sweets and beauties, that fasten the eyes upon it with delight and admiration. Whatever is beautiful or bright, verdant or gay, in heaven and earth, are here collected together, arranged in the most harmonious order, and pleasing not less by their juxtaposition than by their separate traits of loveliness. It is a picture on which the eye could banquet for hours, with an unsated gaze.[52]

This same writer went on to characterize *Expulsion* as being "of a different character" and quoted the concluding lines from Milton's *Paradise Lost* to explain the image.[53] The reviewer also observed that Cole had "succeeded most happily in heightening the principal object of his picture not only by the antithetical disposition of light and shade, but by the skilful contrast of a portion of the garden, still unfaded and lovely, seen on the right of the picture, with the arid, gloomy, and desolate appearance of every thing before the unhappy outcasts." The review concluded: "The two pictures, the Garden and the Expulsion, will contribute a large addition to the fame of the young artist who accomplished them."

Cole must have been pleased by these words of praise. However, on Saturday, June 21, 1828, he found a very different and highly disturbing view of him and his pictures in the *Morning Courier*, by a writer using the pseudonym "Middle-Tint":

> No. 24. Garden of Eden, by J. [*sic*] Cole, N.A. It was our intention this day, to have descanted largely, on the composition and painters [*sic*] of this piece, but beg leave to request a few day's indulgence, till we have made strict inquiry into the fact, *"whether or not this picture was composed by Mr. Cole, or by some other artist,"* as has been bluntly averred. Hints, nay positive assertions have been repeatedly made to us, by his most intimate friends, and members of the National Academy, that the Garden of Eden was copied *"Linea per linea"* from the engraved piece called the PAPHIAN BOWER [see fig. 33]; and that, with the exception of the beast of prey, and one or two little items, the whole of the expulsion is a literal copy of the celebrated MARTIN'S picture [see fig. 34]. If these things be so, we sincerely regret the circumstance that Mr. Cole had not publicly announced the fact – the acknowledgement would have been honorable, and had its due weight in the *public scale of justice*. For ourself, we are almost positive that the composition is not Martin's, but really that of Mr. Cole. We have too high an opinion of the abilities and moral conduct of Mr. Cole to believe him guilty of meanness. From the first, we pronounced our belief of his originality, of his genius. Supposing for an instant that the designs above alluded to were not original, what would it prove? Would it detract from his merits as a colorist? as the most faithful delineator of nature? We adventure to repeat, that at this day, in this western world, he stands unrivalled as a landscape painter.
>
> A few remarks from Mr. Cole, will be most gratifying to his *many friends*, and to us in particular.[54]

Cole can only have been shocked and outraged by this extraordinarily damning notice. The writer, although claiming only to want the issue resolved fairly and all the while cleverly asserting his admiration for Cole and his belief that the artist had done nothing wrong, was accusing the young painter of artistic plagiarism in no uncertain terms.[55] As we have seen, Cole undoubtedly did know Martin's works and was, in part, inspired by them for his two Eden pictures. But he unquestionably regarded his first attempts in "a higher style of landscape" to be independent products that showed his, not any other artist's, abilities to compose complex and elaborate landscapes. His response to "Middle-Tint" was a strongly worded assertion of his innocence:

> I have been charged in one of the public prints, and in the most artful manner, with being a plagiarist. As an artist's reputation is his *all*, I hope you will permit me through the medium of your paper to endeavor to save the little I possess from being wrested from me by the malicious. It is said that my picture of the *Garden of Eden* is a copy of Martin's *Paphian Bower*; and that my *Expulsion* is from a picture by the same distinguished artist; both these charges are false. The print of the *Paphian Bower* is now exhibited by the side of my *Garden of Eden*. Those who will favor me by examining it, will be convinced that the first charge is unfounded. The print from the expulsion is in town, and would have been placed by the side of my picture on the same subject, could it have been obtained. I trust I shall be believed when I say, that my picture was conceived and painted *long before I knew that such a print was in the country*. A single glance at it will show how preposterous is this latter charge.

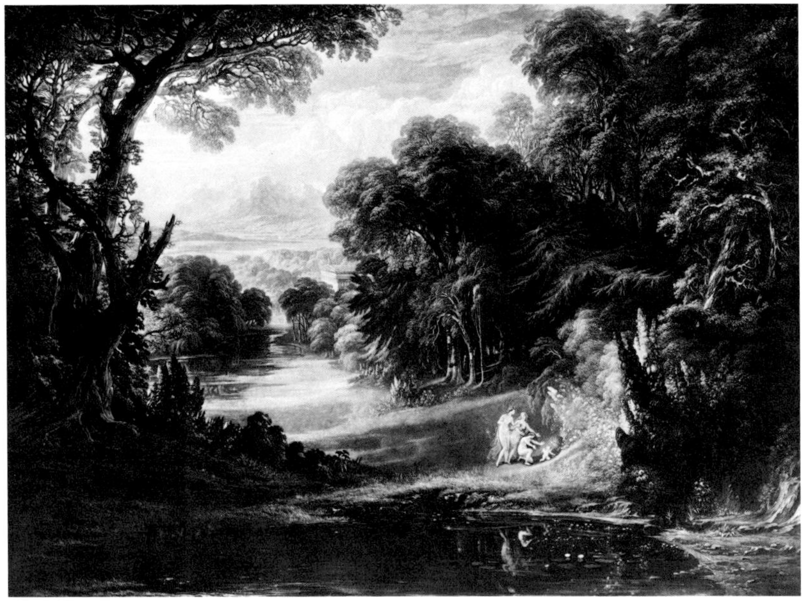

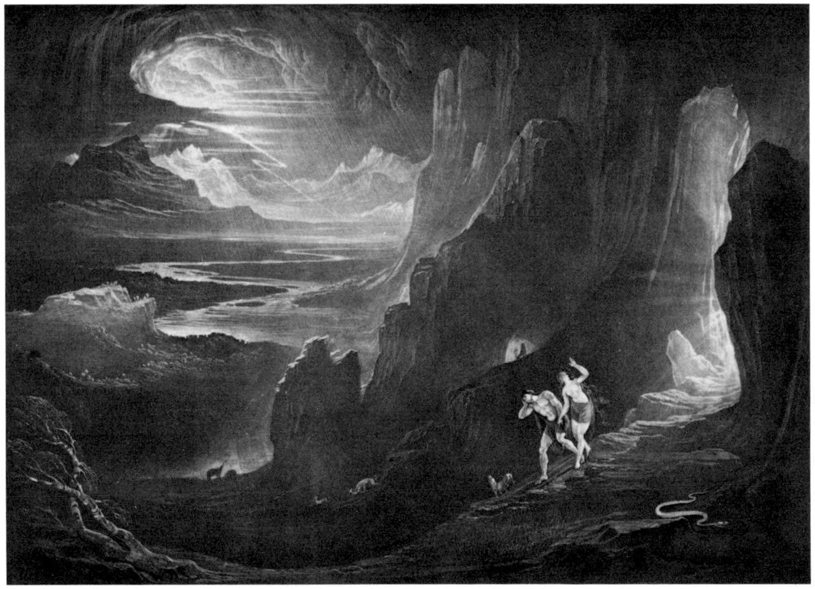

Figure 33 (*top*). George Henry Phillips, after John Martin, *The Paphian Bower*, mezzotint, 1826, plate: 19⁵⁄₁₆ x 25⅝ in., sheet: 20⅝ x 26¾ in., The Metropolitan Museum of Art, New York

Figure 34 (*bottom*). John Martin, *Adam and Eve Driven out of Paradise*, mezzotint proof from John Milton's *Paradise Lost*, 1827, plate: 10 x 13⅞ in., Museum of Fine Arts, Boston

> Not only is my reputation as an artist effected by these misrepresentations, but also my character as a man of veracity; for he who offers to the public as his own, the productions of another, is guilty of falsehood.
>
> Laboring under these slanderous imputations, I hope I shall be excused for thus appearing unwillingly before them.[56]

Recent scholarship on Cole has devoted considerable attention to this incident and has carefully considered whether he could be, by the standards of the time, judged guilty of the wrongs "Middle-Tint" accused him of.[57] Certainly Cole's response was unequivocal, and his decision to hang a copy of Martin's *Paphian Bower* (fig. 33) next to his painting of *The Garden of Eden* must have convinced many of his innocence, for the two works do not look, on the face of it, greatly similar. Some scholars, however, have noted that Cole might not have fared so well if Martin's *Adam and Eve – The Morning Hymn* (see fig. 7) was hung in place of the *Paphian Bower*, or, even more, if a copy of Martin's *Expulsion* (fig. 34) had been available for display. However, it is generally agreed that Cole was working within an established artistic tradition that approved of taking inspiration from the work of others, even to the point of adapting and reforming their ideas to new ends. In short, in an era long before the ascendancy of modernist beliefs about artistic individuality and the complete discarding of the past, it was acceptable, and even expected, that an artist demonstrate in his works an understanding of tradition. In that sense, Cole's Eden pictures were, on the one hand, informed by a world of art that was not bound by the narrow confines of New York and, on the other, original creations that were unlike anything previously seen.

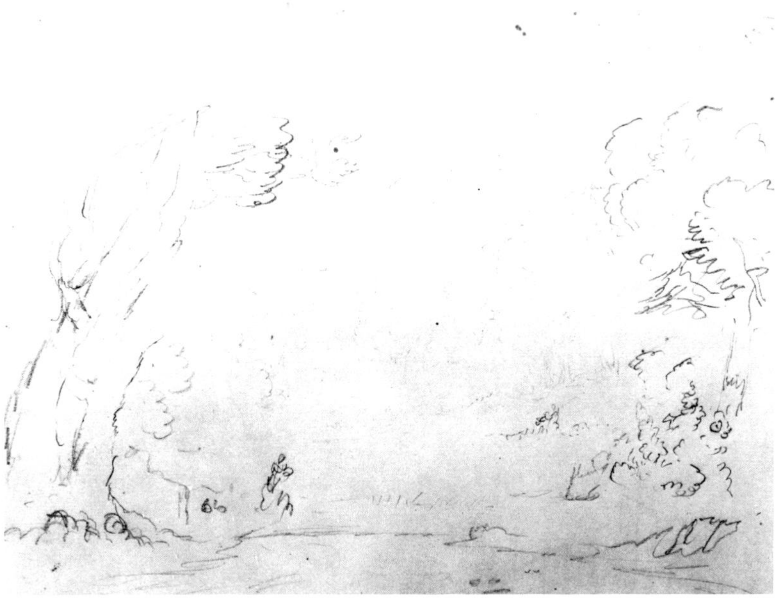

Figure 35. Thomas Cole, Sketchbook page with drawing after *The Paphian Bower*, graphite on paper, 1827/28, 7¾16 x 9⅝ in., New York State Library, Albany, Manuscripts Division

However, one small, but telling, bit of evidence in this story has previously gone unnoticed among the various Eden drawings in Cole's sketchbook. Cole could not very well claim he did not of know Martin's *Paradise Lost* prints at all, for they were certainly available in America at the time of their publication.[58] However, that he was not influenced by the *Paphian Bower* becomes less likely in light of a drawing (fig. 35) on the page immediately preceding Cole's "Memorandum from Pillement" (see fig. 12). Although this drawing is generally faint and somewhat difficult to read, it appears to depict a foreground pool flanked by low underbrush and larger trees in a way that is suggestively similar to Martin's print. That, in itself, would not be conclusive, but there are also remnants of an erased inscription at the top. Although legible only in part, it seems to read: "Memorandum from Martin Paphian Bower from memory." If that is correct, and if this drawing was done during the campaign of work on *The Garden of Eden* (which seems likely) and not later, it would prove that Cole did indeed borrow from Martin's work. His assertion of complete innocence, then, becomes somewhat more difficult to accept uncritically.[59]

Although Cole seems to have weathered the storm caused by "Middle-Tint," the salability of his Eden pictures was surely hurt by such an unpleasant business. This was particularly frustrating, for the artist saw them as a way to raise money for a trip to Europe. Having failed initially in interesting Wadsworth in the pictures, and having turned down an early offer from a Boston collector for *The Garden of Eden*, Cole had been counting on the exposure of the National Academy exhibition to help sell one or both.[60] As Robert Gilmor opined: "I should imagine you would be at no loss to dispose of these pictures in New York, where you have so many rich and thriving men, unless *you set too high a price on them*."[61] But, as Cole sadly wrote to Wadsworth on June 5, 1828:

> Though I have been labouring hard for many months past trusting that by doing so I should accomplish my voyage – I begin to think I shall have to content myself under a disappointment – You know I have spent much time in the execution of the two pictures, the Edens, they are not sold: when I began the first I hardly expected to sell it: but afterwards, owing to the high encomiums it received, I formed higher hopes, and painted another – I was perhaps unwise in taking such subjects, but I felt them, and was led away, without calculating on what I might lose.[62]

The National Academy exhibition closed on July 10, 1828, and by then Cole had already made plans to exhibit the unsold Eden pictures again, this time in Boston.[63] The initial response there was positive, according to a notice in a Boston paper:

> We have been much gratified in viewing a representation of the Garden of Eden in its primeval and happy state – a luxuriant landscape of variegated beauty – the residence of innocent and holy beings. By its side is another view, representing the Expulsion of revolted man, into a world made terrific by tokens of the anger of God. They are paintings of Mr. Cole, of New York . . . worthy, in our opinion, of the patronage of the public and calculated to produce a lasting moral effect on the contemplative beholder.[64]

However, once again Cole would be disappointed. As the artist George Harvey later recalled: "It so happened my friend Cole was at this city . . . exhibiting his pictures of Adam and Eve, and when I met him he wore as lugubrious a face as myself, for his works were not appreciated."[65] In October 1828 Cole wrote Wadsworth again, sounding lugubrious indeed: "My unfortunate pictures of the Garden of Eden (which are not yet disposed of) have been a source of mortification and waste of precious time. I shall leave them in Boston – *I hardly know why*."[66] Increasingly frustrated by his inability to sell the Eden paintings, Cole once again turned to Gilmor:

> I believe you are acquainted with the strong desire I have long had to visit Europe for the purposes of studying the works of the Great Masters, and know the advantages young artists may derive from that study. For a few years past I have laboured unceasingly, that I might obtain means for the accomplishment of my desire; hitherto I have been unsuccessful. . . . Your former favour and kindness have encouraged me to ask if you will assist me. My Garden of Eden and Expulsion are not yet sold. May I venture to propose that you should take them into your hands, and advance me a sum that shall enable me to visit Europe, which sum should be repaid in money, or pictures, *when* and *as* you shall think best.[67]

We can only wonder if Gilmor, who, after all, had always wanted "*real American* scenes" from Cole, was struck by the irony of being asked to take his most completely imaginary works. Whatever the case, Gilmor did not agree and suggested instead that Cole try raffling his paintings in New York. Although Cole initially balked at this idea, by February 1829 he had changed his mind and was attempting to raise eight hundred dollars for the pair by selling forty twenty-dollar tickets.[68] But this, too, proved unsuccessful: "I have failed in my raffle. . . . [I]t is probable my pictures are not worth so much as my vanity has led me to suppose."[69]

After so many disappointments, Cole must have been ready to give up hope on what he called his "Paradise speculations."[70] However, in May 1829, when the pictures were once again on public view – this time at the New York bookstore of Elam Bliss – they at last found buyers. And they were distinguished buyers indeed, both of whom already owned works by Cole. *The Garden of Eden* was sold to Charles Wilkes (1764–1833), president of the Bank of New York, and *Expulsion from the Garden of Eden* went, slightly later, to Dr. David Hosack (1769–1835), a prominent New York physician.[71] Wilkes lent *The Garden of Eden* to an exhibition at the National Academy in 1831, which was apparently the last time the picture was seen in public until its rediscovery. He also allowed James Smillie to make an engraving of it (fig. 36), which appeared as a frontispiece to a Bible published in 1832.[72] *Expulsion from the Garden of Eden* appeared publicly two more times during Cole's lifetime after its sale to Hosack. In 1833 it was included in an exhibition at the American Academy of Fine Arts, where it was judged "very well painted . . . [but] not a good picture,"

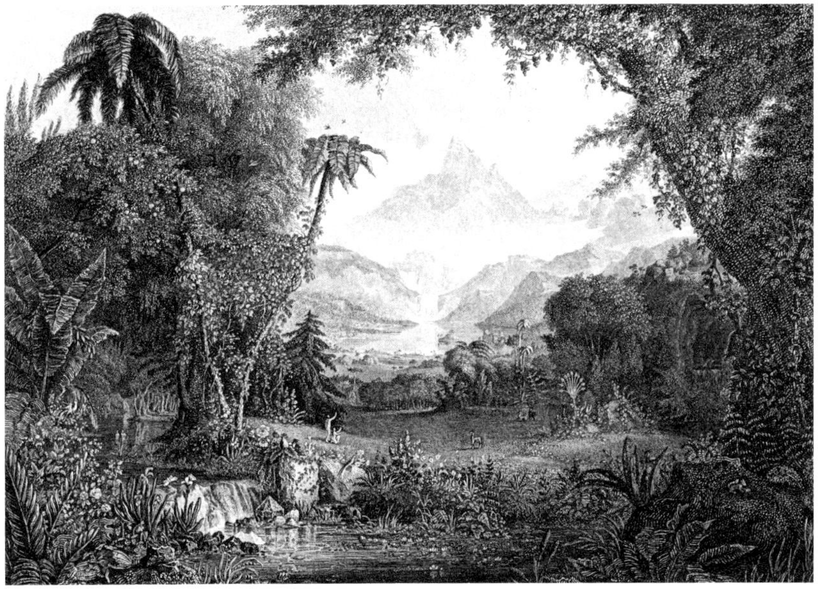

Figure 36. James Smillie, after Thomas Cole, *The Garden of Eden*, engraving, 1831–32, 4 ½ x 6 in., frontispiece for vol. 1 of the Holy Bible (Boston: Gray and Bowen, 1831), New York Public Library, Astor, Lenox and Tilden Foundations

and Cole once again found himself compared to "*Pandemonium* [i.e., John] *Martin*."[73] In 1838 the *Expulsion* appeared in the "Dunlap Benefit Exhibition" at the Stuyvesant Institute in New York, apparently its last appearance in public before the 1848 memorial exhibition of Cole's works.

The Eden Pictures in Context: Meaning and Influence

In the most fundamental way, what Cole's paintings of Eden are about, and what they mean, is perfectly obvious. For anyone familiar with the story of Adam and Eve it would have been manifestly clear that the pictures formed a narrative pair, with *The Garden* representing the world before the fall and the *Expulsion* the world after. And certainly all the attendant lessons about evil, temptation, and original sin could be easily inferred by any viewer who so wished. Cole also seems to have known that certain elements and motifs could carry symbolism that might augment the meaning of his paintings. We would reasonably expect to see many different plants and animals in a picture of the Garden of Eden, as we do in Cole's work. But among the specific examples Cole chose, some had well-established meanings in Christian symbolism, and he may have consciously selected them for that reason.[74] For example, the stag, or hart, which appears so prominently in Cole's painting, was a symbol of the faithful Christian's longing for God. In the *Expulsion*, however, the stag has fallen prey to the hyena, symbolizing the rupture that has occurred between man and the Creator. Flowers and fruit are generally symbolic of the cycles of life and death but also often carry specific meanings. Daisies, for instance, are known as the "eye of God" and symbolize simplicity and innocence, while the columbine is a symbol of sorrow. Among the trees at the right of Cole's painting are various clusters of fruit, which generally represent the bounties of Eden. Some seem to be grapes growing on a vine (an ancient symbol of peace and plenty), and others may be pomegranates (symbols of eternity and fertility). At the left a banana tree stands juxtaposed with a pair of graceful palms across the stream. Both were believed to be among the trees that had grown in Paradise.[75] The banana had long been associated with the Tree of Knowledge of good and evil, and the palm was specifically associated with the Tree of Life, which stood in the very center of the Garden.[76] We may reasonably assume that Cole, through this juxtaposition, was alluding to the impending temptation and fall. Finally, a pair of swans, which mate for life, appears in each painting, symbols of the peaceful bliss and eternal stability of life inside the garden walls.[77]

Perhaps such meanings were all that most of those who saw Cole's paintings of Eden expected of them. Nevertheless, we can still reasonably ask whether the paintings might have held

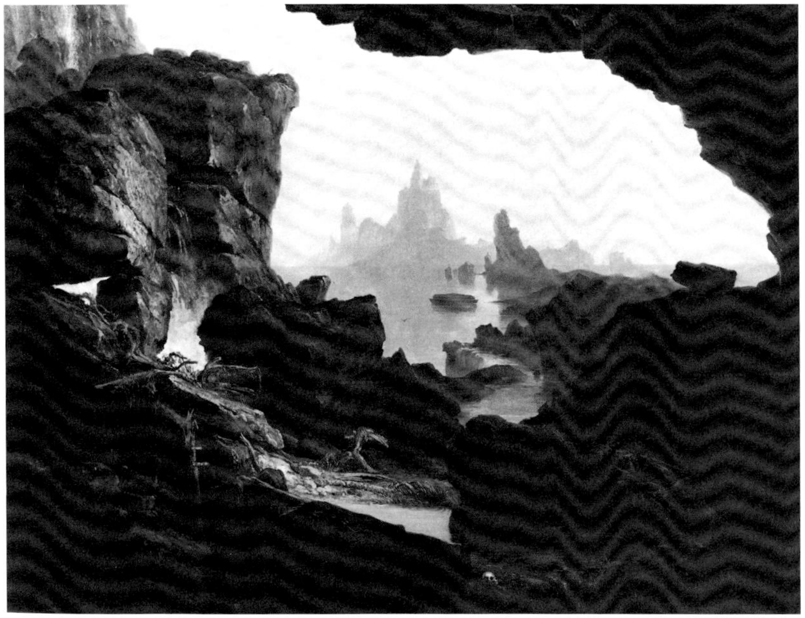

Figure 37. Thomas Cole, *The Subsiding of the Waters of the Deluge*, oil on canvas, 1828, 35¾ x 47⅝ in., National Museum of American Art, Smithsonian Institution, gift of Mrs. Katie Dean in memory of Minnibel S. and James Wallace Dean and museum purchase through the Smithsonian Collections Acquisition Program

additional levels of interpretation for Cole specifically, and for some in his wider audience generally. As we have seen, Cole considered the Eden pictures his first efforts in "a higher style," which he considered far more significant than the simple production of straightforward landscapes. For him, what made such works of greater importance was that they required the artist to use his imagination and mental ability, not just his technical skills. The Eden pictures certainly required all the fresh imagination the young painter could bring to them, but it is also clear that in conceiving them he made use of a time-honored contrast between two types of landscape.[78] On the one hand *The Garden*, with its assemblage of pleasing plants and animals, gentle landscape, and even light, exemplified what was called in aesthetic theory the "Beautiful." The *Expulsion*, on the other hand, with its jagged rocks, chasms, volcano, fighting animals, and stormy sky, represented the more horrific side of nature embodied in the "Sublime." These aesthetic types were, in turn, popularly associated with the lyrical landscapes of Claude Lorrain (1600–1682) and the rocky scenes of Salvator Rosa (1615–1673). By displaying his mastery of Claude's "Beautiful" and Rosa's "Sublime" in works painted from his own imagination, Cole demonstrated that he not only understood the lessons offered by history and tradition but also could create works expressive of his own vision.

The two types of landscape depicted in *The Garden of Eden* and *Expulsion from the Garden of Eden* also can be viewed in the context of contemporary theories about the origins of the earth. As Ellwood Parry has discussed, the tumultuous landscape of the *Expulsion*, with its deep rift, jagged rocks, and erupting volcano, suggests that Cole was well aware that some scientists believed the major features of the earth were the result of past volcanic activity.[79] Generally known as Vulcanists, these men were opposed to the views of their colleagues the Neptunists, who believed that the actions of water (particularly strict believers said the biblical deluge) were responsible for the appearance of the earth. However, even though thus fundamentally disagreeing about the specific mechanisms of geological change, both camps adhered to what was known as catastrophism, which held that violent actions of some kind had formed the surface of the earth. Cole himself seems to have seen the merits of both sides of the theory of catastrophism, for the year after he completed his Eden pictures he painted *The Subsiding of the Waters of the Deluge* (fig. 37), which features an equally dramatic rocky landscape emerging from the receding waters.[80]

Finally, we may also ask whether Cole intended for his Eden pictures to address issues about the identity of the American

Figure 38. Thomas Cole, "Narcissus," pen and black ink heightened with white on paper, 1828, 7¼ x 11½ in., courtesy of Alexander Gallery

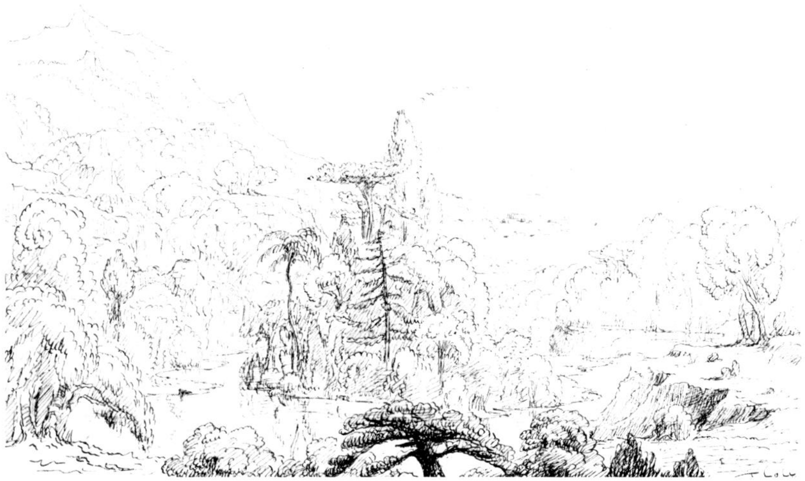

nation itself.[81] There can be, of course, no single myth or belief that explains the origin and development of a complex political and social entity like America. But certainly one of the most persistent ideas in art and literature of the first half of the nineteenth century concerns the identification of America as a new Eden and of Americans as new Adams.[82] If the vast, unspoiled territories of the New World represented not just physically a new Eden but spiritually a place where man could redeem himself, what guarantee was there that Americans might not also fall victim to temptation? That Cole saw the need to create the *Expulsion* as a pendant to his *Garden of Eden* suggests that he wanted to make the ever-present possibility of loss absolutely apparent to his audience. The responsibility, he seemed to say, lay with the individual; as Cole would write: "We are still in Eden; the wall that shuts us out of the Garden is our own ignorance and folly."[83]

Cole never again painted an image of the Garden of Eden, but unmistakable echoes of his early pictures are found in several subsequent works. His 1828 drawing *Narcissus* (fig. 38), presumably an idea for an unrealized painting, shows a verdant landscape with distant mountains that strongly recalls *The Garden of Eden*. His *Dream of Arcadia* (1838, Denver Art Museum), although depicting an imaginary classical past, is also Edenic in character, as are the first two paintings (see figs. 40, 41) from Cole's famous series *The Voyage of Life* (first version, completed 1840, Munson-Williams-Proctor Institute, Utica, N.Y.; second version, completed 1842, National Gallery of Art, Washington, D.C.). Echoes of the *Expulsion*, though perhaps less obvious, can also be found. The now lost painting *Elijah at the Mouth of the Cave* (c. 1829; fig. 39) was surely animated by a

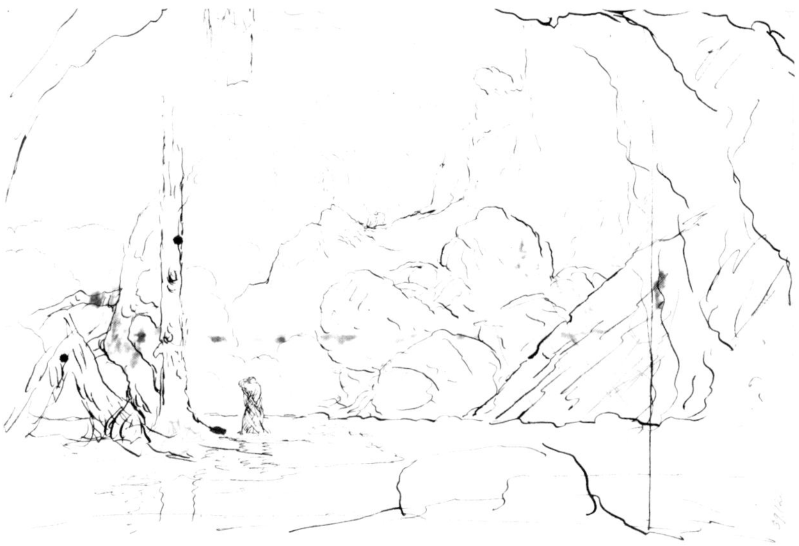

Figure 39. Thomas Cole, Study for *Elijah at the Mouth of the Cave*, pen and ink and graphite on paper, 1828, 9⅞ x 14⁹⁄₁₆ in., Detroit Institute of Arts

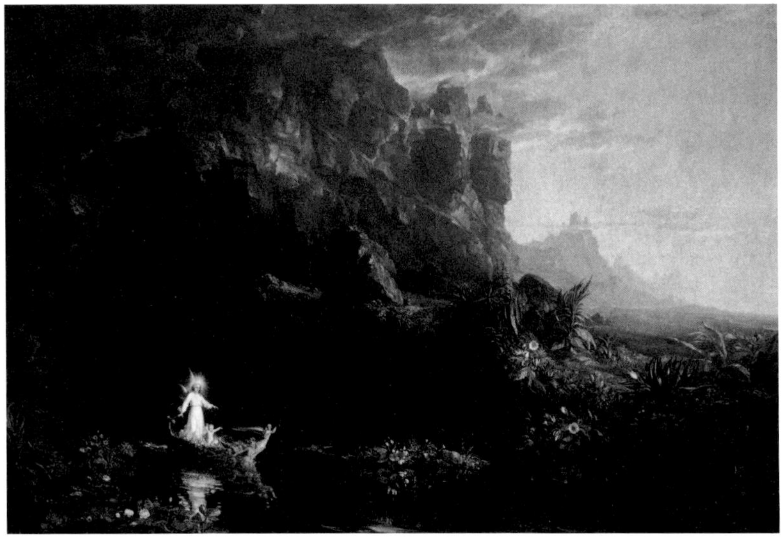

Figure 40. Thomas Cole, *Voyage of Life – Childhood*, oil on canvas, 1842, 52⅞ x 77⅞ in., National Gallery of Art, Washington, Ailsa Mellon Bruce Fund

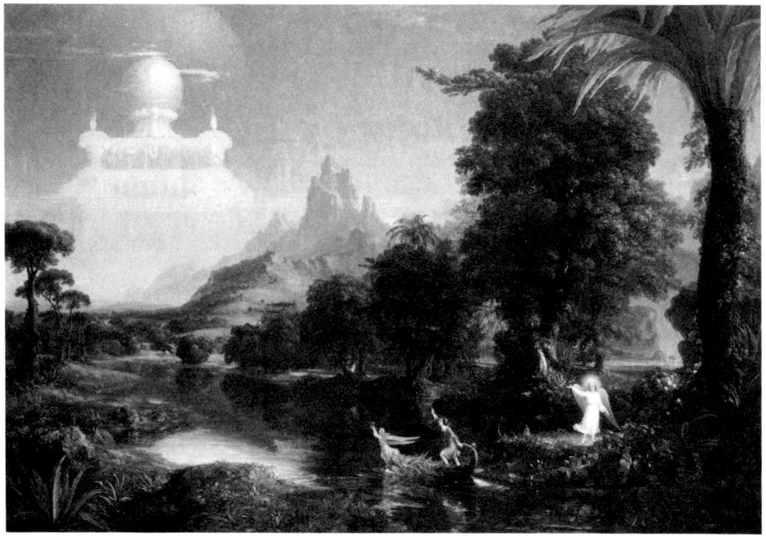

Figure 41. Thomas Cole, *Voyage of Life – Youth*, oil on canvas, 1842, 52⅞ x 76¾ in., National Gallery of Art, Washington, Ailsa Mellon Bruce Fund

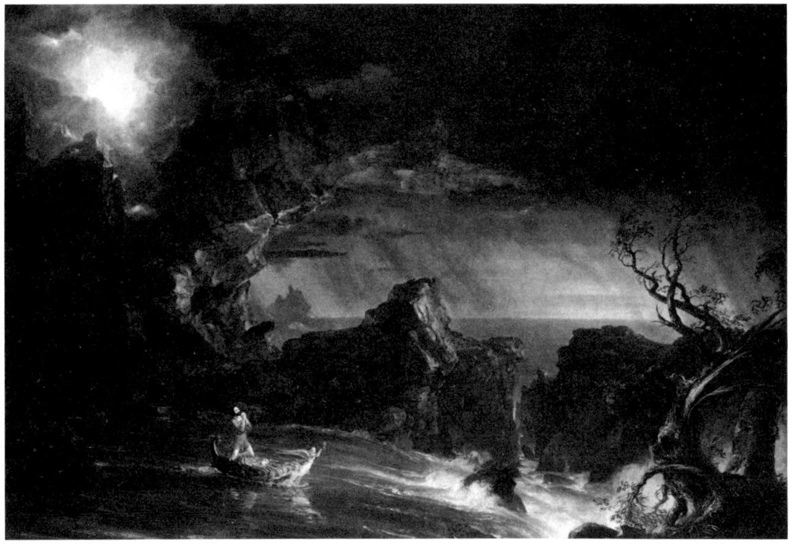

Figure 42. Thomas Cole, *Voyage of Life – Manhood*, oil on canvas, 1842, 52⅞ x 79¾ in., National Gallery of Art, Washington, Ailsa Mellon Bruce Fund

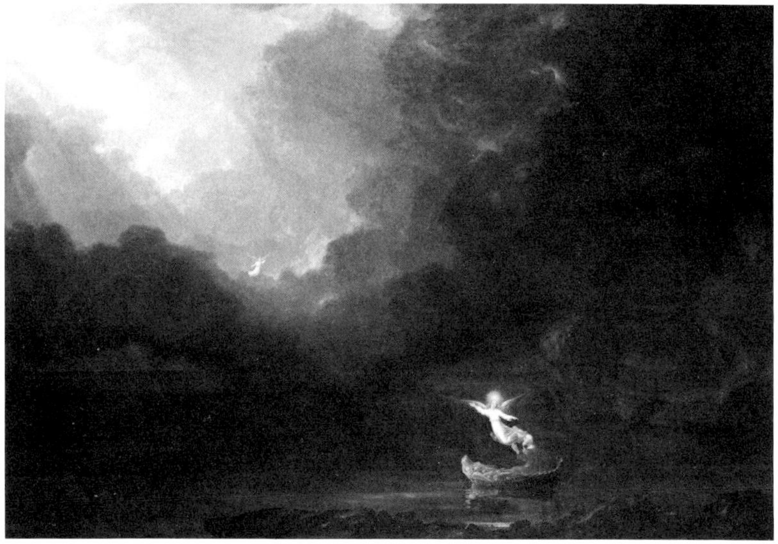

Figure 43. Thomas Cole, *Voyage of Life – Old Age*, oil on canvas, 1842, 52½ x 77¼ in., National Gallery of Art, Washington, Ailsa Mellon Bruce Fund

Figure 44. Charles H. Williamson, photographer, detail of an 1871 installation view showing Thomas Cole's *Pilgrim of the Cross on his Journey*, photograph courtesy of The Brooklyn Historical Society

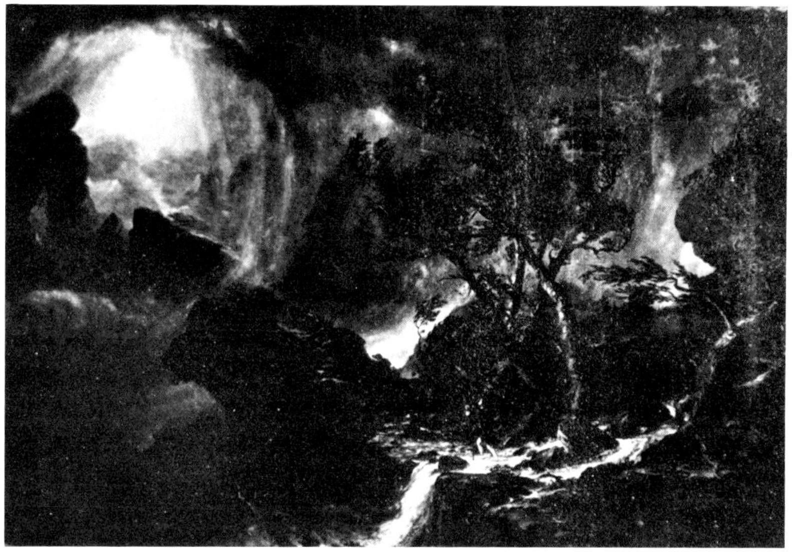

similar mood of geological and meteorological drama. In the vein of pure landscape, Cole's *Tornado* (1833, The Corcoran Gallery of Art, Washington, D.C.), with its blasted trees, stormy sky, and tiny, windblown figure, reads as a kind of naturalized American Expulsion. But it was in Cole's two great moralizing series, *The Voyage of Life* (figs. 40–43) and *The Cross and the World* (unfinished at Cole's death and now known only through sketches and photographs), that the *Expulsion* worked its most noticeable influence. That this was so is hardly surprising, for both of these dealt, in different ways, with man's struggle to overcome the legacy of original sin. In *Manhood* (fig. 42), the third picture from *The Voyage of Life*, the everyman traveler is hopelessly overwhelmed in a chaotic landscape very much like the one that greeted Adam and Eve when they first set foot outside the Garden. And only with death (fig. 43) would the traveler ever escape the meshes of the postlapsarian world. In the same way, the pilgrim of the cross in *The Cross and the World* (fig. 44) must struggle against nature and the elements in his quest to find the cross and salvation. Both series, then, show moments in the unending journey that was first set in motion when Adam and Eve forever lost their place in the Garden of Eden.

Cole's Eden pictures also influenced the works of other artists, although their effect was more gradual, coming primarily after his death.[84] For some artists, such as Jasper Francis Cropsey, who considered his *Spirit of War* (fig. 45) and *Spirit of Peace* (fig. 46) his own "first efforts in this class of art," the possibility of pairing sharply contrasting landscapes was particularly appealing.[85] Others found that Cole's magical re-creation of the very look of Paradise affected them more strongly. Certainly we may imagine that the panorama of the Garden of Eden that Henry Cheever Pratt showed in Boston in 1850, though no longer extant, must have owed more than a little to Cole's example.[86] Pratt, who met Cole in Boston in 1828 while the Eden pictures were there on exhibition, had tried his own effort at a grand biblical landscape in the manner of Cole and Martin in his *Moses on the Mount* (1828–29, Shelburne Museum, Shelburne, Vt.). Pratt described his Eden panorama as "Presenting a vast range of gorgeous scenery, with the most remarkable and beautiful animals, birds, rare and splendid trees, fruits, and flowers of every clime," and listed well over one hundred specific types of trees, plants, and animals depicted. Even Asa Gray, the great Harvard botanist, was impressed.[87] We also can only guess at the appearance of a series of Adam and Eve subjects exhibited in New York in 1865 by Thomas P. Rossiter, who had traveled with Cole in Italy in 1841.[88] However, the second of these, *Morning*, showed "Adam and Eve at the first flush of a cloudless sunrise, contemplating a landscape

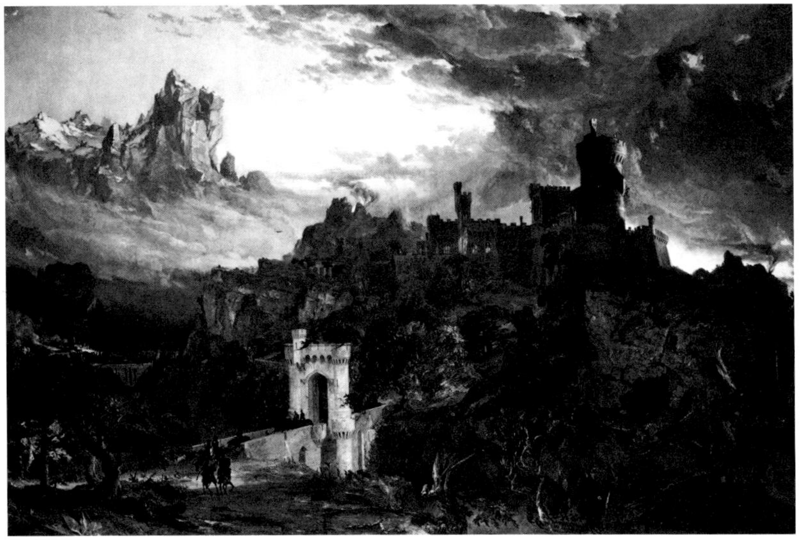

Figure 45. Jasper Francis Cropsey, *The Spirit of War*, oil on canvas, 1851, 43⅝ x 67⅝ in., National Gallery of Art, Washington, Avalon Fund

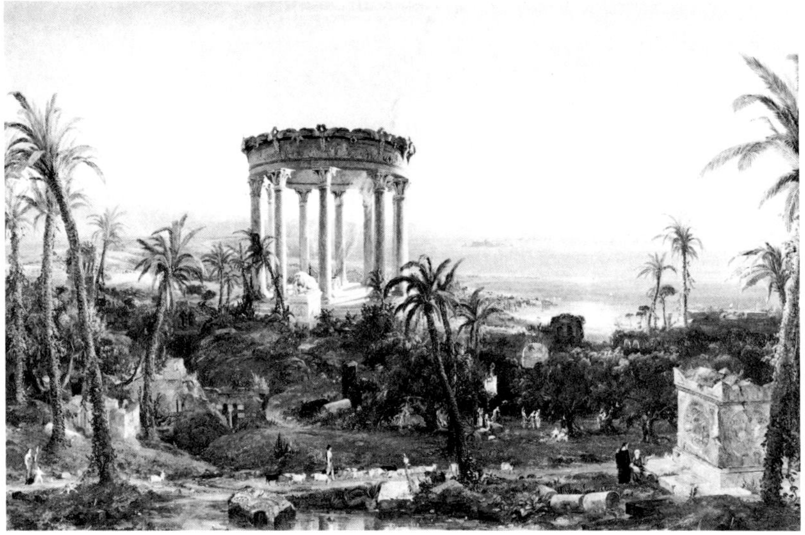

Figure 46. Jasper Francis Cropsey, *The Spirit of Peace*, oil on canvas, 1851, 43¾ x 67⅞ in., Woodmere Art Museum, Philadelphia, Bequest of Charles Knox Smith

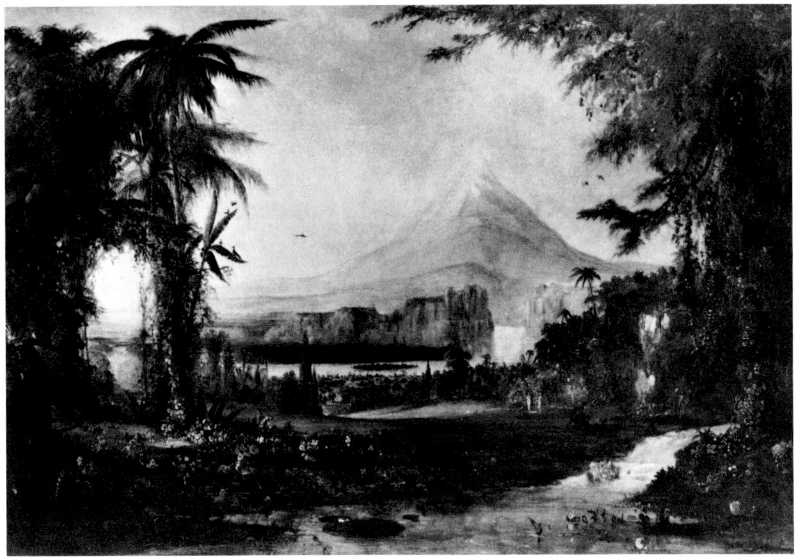

Figure 47. Robert S. Duncanson, *The Garden of Eden*, oil on canvas, 1852, 32¾ x 48 in., West Foundation, on loan to the High Museum of Art, Atlanta

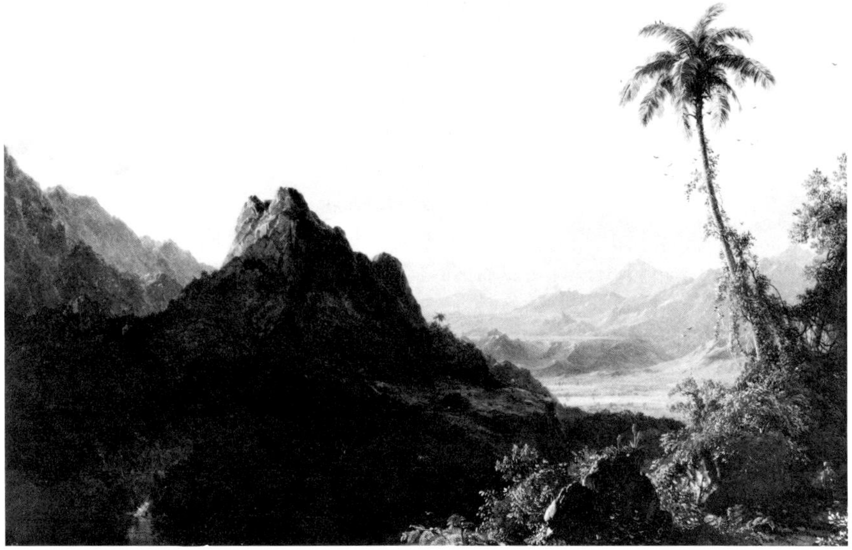

Figure 48. Frederic Church, *In the Tropics*, oil on canvas, 1856, 25¼ x 36¼ in., Virginia Museum of Fine Arts, The Arthur and Margaret Glasgow Fund, photograph © 1990

of varied combination . . . and surrounded by a profusion of tropical foliage, flowers and fruits," which certainly suggests the influence of Cole's prototype.

At least one artist, Cincinnati's Robert Duncanson, painted and exhibited a close copy of Cole's *Garden of Eden* (fig. 47).[89] Although he reversed some elements of the original and changed others, Duncanson clearly had a detailed knowledge of Cole's composition. That knowledge, however, could only have come from the Smillie engraving, for by 1852 the painting itself was inaccessible in a private collection. Indeed, perhaps the greatest variation between Duncanson's Eden and its model is in its color scheme, for the black and white engraving could offer no help in that regard. Duncanson's early study of Cole's *Eden* served him well, for he went on to make an international reputation for imaginary and paradisiacal landscapes such as the immense *Land of the Lotus Eaters* (1861, Collection of the King of Sweden).

But it was perhaps Frederic Edwin Church who learned the most from Cole's vision of Eden and who used that knowledge to help him create works of startling originality. Church studied with Cole in Catskill, New York, in 1844–46 and, more than any other member of the younger generation of landscape painters who matured around 1850, was deeply influenced by his master's belief in "a higher style of landscape." Although he gradually abandoned imaginary paintings by the early 1850s, Church managed to make realistic landscape function in a strongly allegorical way throughout his entire career. Always seeking new and ever more dramatic scenery, Church made two trips to South America in the 1850s. And there he found scenery that must have made him think back to his teacher's images of Eden. Without question, in such masterworks as *The Heart of the Andes* of 1859 (The Metropolitan Museum of Art, New York) Church painted, in exacting, scientifically correct detail, a world that seemed very nearly to be the long-lost Garden of Eden. But in other instances, such as his *Cotopaxi* (1862, The Detroit Institute of Arts), with its dramatic geology and erupting volcano, Church seems to have been thinking not of Paradise regained but of Paradise lost. In fact, when we look at an earlier South American picture such as *In the Tropics* (fig. 48), where the scene is divided between a lush tropical landscape and a rugged, inhospitable region, the prototype that suggests itself most strongly is Cole's *Expulsion*.[90]

In the end, what seems of greatest significance about Cole's Eden pictures is that they were a beginning, "first attempts," as he called them. And like many first attempts to do something ambitious, but also difficult and unprecedented, they did not come into being without struggle. Nor were they received with the unquestioned admiration their creator felt they deserved. Cole's Edens, as we have seen, taxed him intellectually, physically, and emotionally, and failed to reap the expected critical and financial rewards. Without doubt, this bittersweet experience taught the young painter important lessons that were both positive and negative. Cole would be hesitant for the rest of his career to create major works of art without first securing a patron willing to pay for them. But that does not mean he was in any way willing to compromise his ambitions for "a higher style of landscape." *The Garden of*

Eden and *Expulsion from the Garden of Eden* had shown him the rich thematic and pictorial possibilities of serial imagery, and when he returned to New York from Europe late in 1832, he already had in mind what would become his great five-part series, *The Course of Empire* (completed 1836, The New-York Historical Society). Other serial paintings – *Departure* and *Return* (1837, The Corcoran Gallery of Art, Washington, D.C.), *Past* and *Present* (1838, Mead Art Museum, Amherst College, Amherst, Mass.), and *The Voyage of Life* among them – would follow, and it was on these, far more than on his pure landscapes, that Cole felt his strongest claim to fame rested. As one contemporary source said, Cole's deepest and most cherished wish was "to teach the world great truths through the medium of the pictorial art."[91] With his paintings of Eden Cole began, in a remarkably serious and profound way, to bring those truths to light. They were, as his friend George Washington Greene would later observe, "beautiful harbingers of what he was soon to do."[92]

FRANKLIN KELLY

Acknowledgments

In April 1990, when I was in Fort Worth to give a lecture, Doreen Bolger, then the Amon Carter Museum's Curator of Paintings and Sculpture, took me to the conservation laboratory of the Kimbell Art Museum to see a painting that the Carter had recently acquired. Although I had heard rumors that an important nineteenth-century painting had been rediscovered, and had even guessed that it might be Cole's Garden of Eden, *it was still an unforgettable thrill to walk into the lab and see that very picture there before me on the easel. When Doreen and Jan Muhlert subsequently invited me to participate in this exhibition devoted to Cole's paintings of Eden and to write this essay, I happily recalled the exhilaration of that special moment and accepted with pleasure.*

The many scholars, museum professionals, and others who assisted in the organization of the exhibition itself are acknowledged in Jan Muhlert's foreword to this publication; I also am grateful to all of those individuals. With regard to my work on the essay, several people deserve special recognition. As always, the staff of the Amon Carter has assisted me at countless moments, and it has been a pleasure to work with them. Sarah Cash, Assistant Curator of Paintings and Sculpture, who assumed the role of exhibition coordinator from the beginning, has been of immeasurable help. During a time when she was busily organizing her own exhibition devoted to Martin Johnson Heade, she faithfully kept me up to date with information, made travel arrangements, and journeyed with me to visit collections and examine objects. She kept the whole enterprise together and running on schedule, and did it with a great deal of kindness and thorough professionalism. I cannot thank her enough. I was also fortunate to have the assistance of a very gifted researcher, Laurette McCarthy, who had already proven her mettle in working on Thomas Cole with me when she was an intern at the National Gallery of Art. Ms. McCarthy, with diligence and perseverance, tracked down endless bits of information on Cole and his era and cheerfully followed countless leads both useful and not. Her contributions were important to virtually every stage of writing the catalogue essay.

Many others helped me at various points along the way. In particular, I thank Kathie Bennewitz, Emil Bosshard, Ginger Clayton, Thérèse O'Malley, Ken Myers, and Thayer Tolles. Karen Hinson helped with research and, as always, gave general support. My sons Taylor and Jamie, who have grown up knowing Cole's Garden of Eden *from a poster, helped just by being.*

NOTES

1. Cole to Robert Gilmor, Jr., May 21, 1828; quoted in Howard S. Merritt, ed., "Correspondence between Thomas Cole and Robert Gilmor, Jr.," *Studies on Thomas Cole, an American Romanticist* (Baltimore: The Baltimore Museum of Art, 1967), p. 58.

2. Review of Louis L. Noble, *The Voyage of Life, Course of Empire, and Other Pictures of Thomas Cole*, in *North American Review* 77 (October 1853): 316.

3. E. Anna Lewis, "Art and Artists of America: Thomas Cole, N.A.," *Graham's Magazine* 47 (April 1855): 336.

4. "The Artists of America: Thomas Cole," *Crayon* 7 (February 1860): 45–46.

5. In addition to its use as the frontispiece of the Gray and Bowen Bible, the Smillie engraving also exists in loose form. The loose print, like the Bible, is somewhat rare and has been located only in the collections of the New York Public Library and the Albany Institute of History and Art. The impression in the New York Public Library may be a proof for the Bible; under the image it bears the printed text: "Garden of Eden./From the original in the possession of C. Wilks [*sic*] Esqr., New York." It is signed in pencil under the lower right corner of the plate "James Smillie. 1831," and, below that in another hand, "His second Eng. from a painting – The first being after Wien's Covent Gate." In pencil at the lower right corner of the sheet is inscribed: "For a Bible in Boston – Engd for 'Peter Parley' $250-." The uninscribed impression in the Albany Institute is included in a Cole family scrapbook. It bears the same printed text as the impression in the Bible, which consists of the text on the New York impression followed by: "Entered according to Act of Congress. 1832, by S.G. Goodrich in the Clerks Office of the D. Court of Mass." See Mary Alice Mackay, "Annotated Checklist of the Thomas Cole Collections: Albany Institute of History and Art," in *Thomas Cole: Drawn to Nature* (Albany: Albany Institute of History and Art, 1993), p. 106, checklist no. 217 [p. 30].

6. Louis Legrand Noble, *The Life and Works of Thomas Cole* (1853), ed. Elliot S. Vesell (Cambridge, Mass.: Harvard University Press, The Belknap Press, 1964), p. 61.

7. William Dunlap, *A History of the Rise and Progress of the Arts of Design in the United States*, 3 vols. (1834; reprint, Boston: C. E. Goodspeed and Co., 1918), 3:146.

8. See Merritt, "Correspondence," and J. Bard McNulty, ed., *The Correspondence of Thomas Cole and Daniel Wadsworth* (Hartford, Conn.: The Connecticut Historical Society, 1983). Ellwood C. Parry III has traced this period in "Thomas Cole's Early Career: 1818–1829," in Edward J. Nygren, *Views and Visions: American Landscape before 1830* (Washington, D.C.: The Corcoran Gallery of Art, 1986), pp. 161–185.

9. Letter to Cole, December 27, 1826; quoted in Merritt, "Correspondence," p. 47.

10. Gilmor to Cole, December 13, 1826; Cole to Gilmor, December 25, 1826; quoted in Merritt, "Correspondence," pp. 45, 47.

11. Cole to Gilmor, December 25, 1826.

12. Gilmor to Cole, December 27, 1826; quoted in Merritt, "Correspondence," p. 48.

13. Gilmor refers to a "third" picture because he had already commissioned (but not yet received) a companion to *Sunrise in the Catskills*.

14. Cole to Gilmor, January 2, 1827; quoted in Merritt, "Correspondence," p. 50.

15. Gilmor actually believed that he had agreed to buy the *Saint John* as his third picture and wrote to Cole on December 5, 1827, enquiring when he might expect to receive it. Cole claimed to have forgotten their arrangement; see Merritt, "Correspondence," pp. 50–54.

16. Parry, "Cole's Early Career," p. 178.

17. Gilmor to Cole, December 13, 1827; quoted in Merritt, "Correspondence," p. 56.

18. See Ellwood C. Parry III, "Acts of God, Acts of Man: Geological Ideas and the Imaginary Landscapes of Thomas Cole," in Cecil J. Schneer, ed., *Two Hundred Years of Geology in America* (Hanover, N.H.: University Press of New England, 1979), pp. 57–58.

19. On Cole's list, see Howard S. Merritt, "Thomas Cole's List: 'Subjects for Pictures,'" in *Studies on Thomas Cole*, pp. 82–101. Merritt (p. 84) found Cole's written description "too faint to read clearly" and included only up to the words "nearer Plains with." The transcription given here, made by Sarah Cash and Franklin Kelly working from Cole's original list, is of the entire inscription.

20. Quoted in McNulty, *Correspondence*, p. 20. Ellwood C. Parry, *The Art of Thomas Cole: Ambition and Imagination* (Newark, Del.: University of Delaware Press, and London and Toronto: Associated University Presses, 1988), p. 70, reasonably suggests that Cole was in this letter attempting to interest Wadsworth in commissioning the painting.

21. McNulty, *Correspondence*, p. 20; John Milton, *Paradise Lost* (1674), ed. William G. Madsen (New York: The Modern Library, 1969), pp. 99–100.

22. January 2, 1827; quoted in Merritt, "Correspondence," p. 50.

23. This painting and a companion canvas, *The Dead Abel*, were sold by the Academy in 1989; see auction sale, *Important Paintings by Old Masters*, Christie's, New York, January 11, 1989, pp. 106-107, attributed to Antonio Molinari and Antonio Balestra, respectively.

24. Robert Gilmor in a letter to Cole of May 24, 1828 (Merritt, "Correspondence," p. 59), mentioned the Flemish painter: "the subjects are both trying ones, particularly the *Garden of Eden*, which would require the skillful execution of the figures & animals, to be found chiefly in Breughel." However, contrary to what is stated in Doreen Bolger and Kathleen Motes Bennewitz, "Thomas Cole's *Garden of Eden*," *Antiques* 138 (July 1990): 107, Cole himself did not cite Brueghel as one of his sources. F. W. H. Hollstein, *Dutch and Flemish Etchings, Engravings and Woodcuts*, 41 vols. (Amsterdam: M.Hertzberger, 1951), 3:252, lists one print after a Brueghel image of Eden (James Heath, *Adam and Eve in Paradise*, 1799; however there is no mention of this print in John Heath, *The Heath Family of Engravers, 1779–1878* [Aldershot, England: Scolar Press, 1993], which includes a catalogue raisonné of Heath's prints). There is no evidence that Cole saw this print, but the possibility cannot be excluded.

There was a major example of Brueghel's work – *Paradise Landscape with the Animals Entering Noah's Ark* (1613, now in the J. Paul Getty Museum, Santa Monica) – in a private collection in Maryland by the 1820s, but it is extremely unlikely Cole could have seen it, for he had not visited Maryland, and the painting seems not to have been exhibited publicly.

25. Christopher Johnstone, *John Martin* (London and New York: Academy Editions, 1974), p. 111.

26. On these see J. Dustin Wees, *Darkness Visible: The Prints of John Martin* (Williamstown, Mass.: Sterling and Francine Clark Art Institute, 1986), pp. 18–19.

27. Cole to Gilmor, December 25, 1826; quoted in Merritt, "Correspondence," p. 47.

28. Cole to Gilmor, December 27, 1826.

29. Parry, "Cole's Early Career," p. 180, has noted the similarity of the mountain in the *Garden* to Chocorua.

30. Parry, "Cole's Early Career," p. 163.

31. At least one source, "Thomas Cole," *National Magazine* 4 (April 1854): 313, does, however, suggest that Cole made drawings in the tropics: "In his leisure moments he busied himself in sketching the island."

32. *Saturday Evening Post* (Philadelphia), May 14, 1825.

33. "Cole," *National Magazine*, p. 313.

34. I am grateful to Thérèse O'Malley for providing me with information about Elgin Gardens and other early botanical collections in the United States. Dr. David Hosack, one of the founders of Elgin Gardens, would in 1829 purchase Cole's *Expulsion from the Garden of Eden*.

35. (London, 1822; reprint, Westport, Conn.: Negro Universities Press, 1970). Copland's description of the Tevartna tree (p. 322) – "it grows in a pyramidal shape, the branches representing seven distinct stories" – is obviously similar to Cole's words on his drawing (see fig. 10). His description of the Fonti (p. 325), "a plant that grows like a plume of feathers," is also echoed in Cole's "a tree that resembles a bunch of feathers." However, Copland's description of the "Raven Palm" (p. 328) does not seem sufficiently detailed to have allowed Cole to draw it; he thus presumably either found an actual specimen or consulted some other written source with an illustration.

36. Cole probably borrowed the use of the term *memorandum* from William Oram's *Precepts and Observations on the Art of Colouring in Landscape Painting* (London: White and Cochrane, 1810), passages of which he copied in this same sketchbook. Three illustrations in Oram's book use the word *memorandum* in their titles; one is called "Memorandum of a Picture by Nicholas Poussin." Alan Wallach has discussed Cole's interest in Oram in "The Ideal American Artist and the Dissenting Tradition: A Study of Thomas Cole's Popular Reputation" (Ph.D. diss., Columbia University, 1973), pp. 187–189. See also his essay in William H. Truettner and Alan Wallach, eds., *Thomas Cole: Landscape into History* (Washington, D.C.: National Museum of American Art, 1994), pp. 27–28, which appeared after this essay was completed.

37. See Paul Mitchell, "Jean Pillement Revalued," *Apollo* 117 (January 1983): 46–49.

38. Robert Gilmor owned a "River Scene" by Pillement, but it, oddly enough, was "in the style of Salvator Rosa"; see Dunlap, *History of the Arts of Design*, 3:273.

39. Quoted in McNulty, *Correspondence*, p. 33.

40. See also Merritt, "Cole's List," p. 85, where the word "walls" is given as "masses."

41. Cole to Wadsworth, April 11, 1828; quoted in McNulty, *Correspondence*, p. 37.

42. Parry, *Cole*, p. 73.

43. Because several of these drawings are in an intact sketchbook, it might be assumed that the sequence of their execution would correspond to the order of the pages. Perhaps that was so, but there is no evidence in this particular sketchbook, nor in others still intact, that Cole methodically used each page in order.

44. See Howard S. Merritt, *To Walk with Nature: The Drawings of Thomas Cole* (Yonkers, N.Y.: The Hudson River Museum, 1982), p. 30. This rock formation also inspired the passage (at the far left) that Gilmor found so troubling in his version of "*The Last of the Mohicans*" (see fig. 2).

45. This drawing has been discussed by Ellwood Parry in "Thomas Cole and the Practical Application of Landscape Theory," *New Mexico Studies in the Fine Arts* 3 (1978): 17. Parry, however, relates it to the finished canvas in Boston and also reads the outermost ring's inscription as "blue" rather than "mauve."

46. These colors also are similar, although somewhat less obviously, to those found in the finished picture.

47. Parry, *Cole*, p. 75, also feels that this picture is an intermediary version of the Expulsion theme. However, Kenneth W. Maddox, in his entry on the painting in Barbara Novak, ed., *The Thyssen-Bornemisza Collection* (London: Sotheby's Publications, 1986), pp. 58-61, although relating it to the "bridge-of-fear" drawings, suggests it was a "sequential development" of the work now in Boston. Although this possibility cannot be excluded, it seems more likely the painting represents Cole's first attempt at depicting the Expulsion. It should be noted, however, that the present dimensions of the canvas are slightly smaller than *The Garden of Eden*, but it is unclear whether it has been substantially cut down. In a letter to the author of May 13, 1992, Emil Bosshard, Head of Conservation for the Thyssen-Bornemisza Foundation, notes that the painting is no longer on its original stretcher and

has lost its tacking margins all around, making it impossible to know its original size. He did not feel, however, that the painting is presently much smaller than it was originally.

48. Cole's visit to the island of Saint Eustatia had acquainted him with volcanic scenery. As he wrote in "Emma Moreton": "a soft blaze of light was beginning to spread over the summit of the lofty mountain, as the moon slowly rose behind its dark body; and a wild imagination might have supposed that the volcanic fires were again lighting up the blasted rocks, and that the evil spirit of the mountain was again raging in the deep crater."

49. McNulty, *Correspondence*, p. 38.

50. Cole to Wadsworth, April 23, 1828; quoted in McNulty, *Correspondence*, p. 38. Cole's defense of the cave is interesting, for he apparently decided to add it fairly late in the creation of the picture; there is no hint of it in the two compositional drawings (see figs. 17, 18), and technical evidence (see Claire Barry's essay) suggests it was painted over an area that Cole had not dried sufficiently.

51. The two pictures were listed in the exhibition catalogue as:

> 24 Garden of Eden, a composition.
>
> "Lowly they bow'd adoring, and began
> "Their orisons, each morning duly paid
> "In various style;" *Milton*
>
> 115 Expulsion from the Garden of Eden,
>
> "They, looking back, all th'eastern side beheld
> "Of Paradise, so late their happy seat,
> "Wav'd over by that flaming brand,
> * * * * * * *
> "The world was all before them, where to choose
> "Their place of rest, and Providence their guide:
> "They, hand in hand, with wand'ring steps and slow,
> "Through Eden took their solitary way. – Milton.

See *The Exhibition of the National Academy of Design, The Third* (New York: National Academy of Design, 1828), pp. 6, 9. Both works were listed "For sale." As the catalogue numbers indicate, the two works were not hung together; however, the academy exhibitions in these early years did appear in a single gallery. That the two pictures were not hung together probably went against Cole's intentions, for he surely would have preferred them displayed side by side. However, space and wall position were at a premium at the academy, and decisions about placement were made by a hanging committee, not by individual artists. As was stated in the catalogue preface: "The committee have truly had a very difficult and delicate task in apportioning the few good places so impartially among the numerous exhibitors, that each might share equally with his compeers, and at the same time in preserving that symmetry, and proper regard to the effect of the whole, which is indispensable in exhibitions of this kind."

52. "National Academy of Arts and Design," *New-York Mirror and Ladies' Literary Gazette*, May 24, 1828, p. 367.

53. This critic drew from the same passage in Book 12 of *Paradise Lost* as did Cole, but quoted it more fully:

> – – – -High in front advanced,
> The brandished sword of God before them blazed
> Fierce as a comet; which with torrid heat,
> And vapour as the Libyan air adust,
> Began to parch that temperate clime: – –
> Our lingering parents – – -
> – – – -looking back, all th'eastern side beheld
> Of Paradise, so late their happy seat,
> Waved over by that flaming brand, the gate
> With dreadful faces thronged and fiery arms
> The world was all before them, where to choose
> Their place of rest, and Providence their guide,
> They, hand in hand, with wandering steps, and slow,
> Through Eden took their solitary way.

54. "Middle-Tint, on the Works of Living Artists, at the National Academy of Design, No. 5," *Morning Courier* (New York), June 21, 1828. This important review and Cole's subsequent response are discussed in Christopher Kent Wilson, "Rediscovered Thomas Cole Letter: New Light on the *Expulsion from the Garden of Eden*," *American Art Journal* 18 (1986): 73–74. On this controversy, see also Parry, *Cole*, pp. 73–75.

55. As Wilson ("Rediscovered Cole Letter," p. 74) has shown, the author ("Middle-Tint") was almost certainly the New York sculptor John Browere, a member and strong proponent of the American Academy, who regarded the National Academy as an upstart rival institution. His attack on Cole was thus an attempt both to tarnish one of the National Academy's brightest stars and to wound the institution itself.

56. This letter was first published in the *American* on June 23, 1828, and subsequently appeared in the *Morning Courier* on June 24; see Wilson, "Rediscovered Cole Letter," p. 73.

57. See, in particular, Wilson, "Rediscovered Cole Letter," pp. 73–74, and Parry, *Cole*, pp. 73–75.

58. The publisher who commissioned the prints, Septimus Prowett, was, in fact, an American (Johnstone, *Martin*, p. 111). Even though the prints were primarily directed at the British audience, the wide following in America for Milton would have guaranteed healthy sales here as well.

59. That the inscription on this drawing was erased raises, of course, the interesting question of whether it was Cole who erased it and, if so, whether he did it after reading "Middle-Tint's" accusations. It does not, however, seem likely we will ever know the answer.

60. In a letter to Gilmor of January 20, 1829 (Merritt, "Correspondence," p. 62), Cole sadly related how he had missed selling the first picture: "I will endeavor to explain the circumstances of my refusal of $500 for the Garden of Eden. Immediately before the exhibition of last Spring Mr. Goodrich of Boston made me the offer, but wished to have the picture exhibited at the Boston Athenaeum, which was to open shortly; this I refused, and lost the sale of it. It had all along been my wish to have it first exhibited in New-York, and at the time Mr. Goodrich was here bargaining for the picture there had been a place left for it in the gallery of the Academy of Design, and I had long before made them the promise of it." Cole concluded: "I certainly acted very foolishly on this occasion, and it will be a lesson for me in the future."

61. Gilmor to Cole, May 24, 1828; quoted in Merritt, "Correspondence," p. 59.

62. Cole to Wadsworth, June 5, 1828; quoted in McNulty, *Correspondence*, p. 42.

63. Parry, *Cole*, p. 80.

64. "Garden of Eden," *Boston Recorder and Religious Telegram*, August 22, 1828, p. 135.

65. Letter to Charles Lanman, August 13, 1852, formerly collection of E. Maurice Bloch; quoted in *Kindred Spirits, Part II: Manuscripts, Letters and Sketchbooks*, sale catalogue (Boston: ars libri, 1992), p. 38.

66. Cole to Wadsworth, October 13, 1828; quoted in McNulty, *Correspondence*, p. 46.

67. Cole to Gilmor, January 5, 1829; quoted in Merritt, "Correspondence," p. 60.

68. Cole to Gilmor, February 18, 1829; quoted in Merritt, "Correspondence," p. 64.

69. Cole to Gilmor, April 20, 1829; quoted in Merritt, "Correspondence," p. 65.

70. Cole to Wadsworth, undated draft letter, probably April 1829; quoted in McNulty, *Correspondence*, p. 54.

71. Both Wilkes and Hosack were, ironically in light of the incident with "Middle-Tint," stalwart members of the old American Academy of Fine Arts; see Alan Wallach, "Thomas Cole and the Aristocracy," *Arts Magazine* 56 (December 1981): 101.

72. On this engraving, its precise date, and the publication of the Bible, see n.5 above and Bolger and Bennewitz, "Cole's *Garden of Eden*," p. 110.

73. "American Academy of the Fine Arts," *American Monthly Magazine* 6 (August 1, 1833): 402.

74. See Gertrude Grace Sill, *A Handbook of Symbols in Christian Art* (New York: Macmillan Publishing, 1975).

75. See John Prest, *The Garden of Eden: The Botanic Garden and the Re-Creation of Paradise* (New Haven and London: Yale University Press, 1981), pp. 66–86.

76. Prest, *Garden of Eden*, pp. 78–81; see also Katherine Manthorne, "The Quest for a Tropical Paradise: Palm Tree as Fact and Symbol in Latin American Landscape Imagery, 1850–1875," *Art Journal* 44 (Winter 1984): 376–377.

77. A pair of swans also appears in *The Morning Hymn* from Martin's *Paradise Lost* series (see fig. 7).

78. See Parry, "Cole and the Application of Landscape Theory," pp. 15–17.

79. Parry, "Acts of God, Acts of Man," pp. 59–61; on Cole's interest in geology, see also Franklin Kelly, "Myth, Allegory, and Science: Thomas Cole's Paintings of Mount Etna," *Arts in Virginia* 23 (1983): 2–17.

80. As Parry has shown, Cole eventually shifted his allegiance to the view of Sir Charles Lyell, whose theory of uniformitarianism posited that geological change was gradual, not sudden, and spanned eons of time.

81. There are, to be sure, other ways that the Eden pictures could be (and have been) interpreted. For example, Bryan Jay Wolf, in *Romantic Re-vision: Culture and Consciousness in Nineteenth-Century American Painting and Literature* (Chicago and London: University of Chicago Press, 1982), devoted considerable attention to unravelling meaning in the Eden paintings (especially *Expulsion*) by using the psychoanalytic theories of Freud and Jacques Lacan. One might also consider the paintings in the broader context of Milton's influence on American political, social, and cultural beliefs. The literature on this subject is indeed vast, but see most recently Lydia Dittler Schulman, *Paradise Lost and the Rise of the American Republic* (Boston: Northeastern University Press, 1992).

On the relationship between Cole's paintings and issues of national identity, the most recent discussion is found in Angela Miller, *The Empire of the Eye: Landscape Representation and American Cultural Politics, 1825–1875* (Ithaca and London: Cornell University Press, 1993), pp. 49–64.

82. See the now classic text by R. W. B. Lewis, *The American Adam: Innocence, Tragedy and Tradition in the Nineteenth Century* (Chicago: University of Chicago Press, 1955); see also

Frederic I. Carpenter, "'The American Myth': Paradise (To Be) Regained," *Publications of the Modern Language Association of America* 74 (December 1959): 599–606.

83. "Essay on American Scenery," *Atlantic Monthly* (January 1836); reprinted in John W. McCoubrey, *American Art, 1701-1960: Sources and Documents* (Englewood Cliffs, N. J.: Prentice-Hall, 1965), pp. 98–110.

84. John K. Howat, "The Thomas Doughty Exhibition," *American Art Review* 1 (January-February 1974): 100, 106, suggests that Thomas Doughty's turn to more imaginary compositions in late 1828 may have been occasioned by his knowledge of Cole's paintings.

85. On these see Franklin Kelly, *Jasper Francis Cropsey: "The Spirit of War" and "The Spirit of Peace"* (Washington, D.C.: National Gallery of Art, 1994).

86. *Pratt's Great Botanical & Poetical Panorama of the Garden of Eden: as Described in Milton's Paradise, and Immense Moving Mirror of Nature!*, broadside (Boston, 1850).

87. Gray's praise for the panorama was included at the bottom of the broadside.

88. James L. Yarnall and William H. Gerdts, *The National Museum of American Art's Index to American Art Exhibition Catalogues from the Beginning Through the Year 1876*, 6 vols. (Boston: G. K. Hall, 1986), 4:3051.

89. On this painting see Joseph D. Ketner, *The Emergence of the African-American Artist: Robert S. Duncanson* (Columbia and London: University of Missouri Press, 1993), pp. 42–44. The painting now in the West Foundation collection is Duncanson's second and smaller version; the first, according to Ketner, was five by seven feet and was toured by the artist around the Midwest in the summer of 1852.

90. See Franklin Kelly, "Frederic Church in the Tropics," *Arts in Virginia* 27 (1987): 29. When I first proposed this relationship between Church's South American pictures and Cole's *Expulsion*, I was unaware that Bryan Jay Wolf had already presented a similar argument in his "Grammar of the Sublime, or Intertextuality Triumphant in Church, Turner, and Cole," *New Literary History* 16 (Winter 1985): 321–341.

91. "Thomas Cole," *National Magazine* 4 (April 1854): 3219.

92. *Biographical Studies* (New York: G. P. Putnam, 1860), p. 95.

"Painting in Imagination": The Creation of *The Garden of Eden* by Thomas Cole

THE REDISCOVERY OF *The Garden of Eden* by Thomas Cole offered an opportunity to study the artist's most ambitious early work. Painted by the twenty-seven-year-old artist in New York just two years after his arrival in the city, *The Garden* represents Cole's first important attempt at "painting in imagination," composing the landscape entirely in the studio from a handful of preliminary sketches, studies, and color notes. He wrote to his patron Daniel Wadsworth on November 26, 1827: "I am now painting in imagination a scene which I intend embodying on canvas for the next exhibition – the subject is an extremely arduous one . . . the Garden of Eden is the subject."[1] The landscape reveals the technical merits as well as deficiencies of a gifted, young, and self-taught artist on a meteoric rise to fame, and the 1990 examination and subsequent restoration of *The Garden* have yielded a great deal of information about Cole's original intentions, early working methods, and materials.

When the Amon Carter Museum acquired *The Garden of Eden* in 1990, the painting's surface was largely preserved intact under substantial layers of dirt, cloudy yellowed varnish, and discolored retouching. *The Garden*, which had been owned privately since the artist sold it to the New York banker Charles Wilkes in May 1829, had been neglected for several generations. Thus, although it did not suffer from multiple cleanings and unwarranted restoration, unstable environmental conditions had caused paint cleavage to develop and to continue. This had resulted in nine small losses in the upper right quadrant of the picture. The paint film had become so desiccated and fragile that even the most superficial cleaning would have caused further loss of pigment. At some point the painting had been glue lined and presumably cleaned and revarnished. Judging from the extremely discolored varnish, as well as the more recent flake losses, this restoration occurred decades ago. There were also areas of clumsy overpaint on the right side of the landscape and darkened retouching in craquelure along the right and left edges. These restorations as well as the opaque varnish made an accurate assessment of the painting's condition difficult prior to cleaning.

The challenge of restoring a fragile painting of this importance was also complicated by the lack of archival tools that restorers rely on. No written treatment reports or photographs documenting *The Garden*'s condition or earlier appearance were available, nor have previous photographs of the painting been found. James Smillie's 1831 engraving after the finished painting (see Kelly, fig. 36) is the only known image of *The Garden* prior to 1990 – and it was available only in a rare edition of the Bible.[2] Believed to be a faithful record of the painting's appearance shortly after Cole completed it, this engraving is reproduced in numerous books on Cole. For the restoration of *The Garden*, however, it was imperative to study the print firsthand to read accurately the full richness of detail, particularly in the darker passages. Even though it does not record Cole's palette and, characteristic of works in this medium, heightens the contrast and linearity of compositional elements, the engraving still proved invaluable in clarifying details that had become obscured under layers of opaque varnish and overpaint. The Museum borrowed the Bible with Smillie's engraving and made enlarged detail black and white photographs of this print to further elucidate crucial areas of the landscape.

The technical examination of *The Garden* began even before the Bible was in hand. X-radiography revealed that the entire cave area had developed "alligatoring," an extreme form of shrinkage cracking that resulted from contraction of the upper layers of medium-rich paint. This type of cracking usually develops when media containing oil varnish or asphalt underlie the upper paint layers, but it may also result from overpainting layers not yet dry to the touch. In the case of *The Garden*, the "islands" of original paint between interlacing breaks have not only contracted but have also increased in thickness and consequently have wrinkled.[3]

Throughout *The Garden*, less extreme drying craquelure had formed principally in the greens and darks, perhaps as a result of Cole's use of fine-grained pigments, such as ivory black or emerald green, that require a great deal of medium. Similar drying cracks formed throughout the greens and foliage in Cole's painting *The Pastoral* or *Arcadian State* of 1834 (The New-York Historical Society, New York) from his series *The Course of Empire*. In both *The Garden* and *Arcadian State*, this fine network of drying cracks formed in green and dark areas that were unmixed with body color or white.

However, Cole's painting technique may also have contributed to these drying cracks. He built up the surface of *The Garden* to an almost obsessive degree of completion – embroidering the surface with layer upon layer of minute, almost microscopic details such as flowers, foliage, and animals, even insects. It is not surprising that his building up the surface with layers of paint – perhaps without allowing for sufficient drying time – resulted in drying cracks. Finally, applying a varnish layer too early can also lead to drying cracks.[4] In *The Garden*, drying craquelure varies from very fine, almost imperceptible lines throughout the landscape to wider cracks in the cave area.[5] This type of craquelure occurs during the drying process – anywhere from hours to decades after the paint layers were applied and as a direct result of Cole's painting technique. But these should be distinguished from the normal age cracks that appear in the sky and mountains; formed after the painting dried, the age cracks are fine, sharp, and less visually distracting than drying cracks.[6]

The wide drying cracks had rendered Cole's treatment of the cave largely illegible, and a previous restorer had failed to interpret the area as the artist intended, apparently because of ignorance of the painting's original appearance. The cracks were concealed by formless layers of dark retouching, which converted the cave into a shadowy recess with vague areas of foliage. The cave area in *The Garden* likely developed alligatoring because Cole reworked this passage, altering his initial conception of the composition and applying medium-rich paint on top of areas that had not yet dried sufficiently.

In his first letter to Wadsworth about *The Garden*, on November 26, 1827, Cole referred to "umbrageous recesses" but made no specific reference to a cave.[7] Even the most detailed of his preliminary sketches for *The Garden* (see Kelly, figs. 14 and 15) do not include this feature. Initially, Cole had planned a tranquil lake with a forested hill rising behind it. His scraping down and reworking of the cave area, possibly fairly late in his creation of *The Garden*, signaled a major rethinking of a critical element in the composition. He clearly imbued the detail with tremendous significance and defended his choice of motif. Cole wrote to Wadsworth again on April 23, 1828, after the patron had visited him in his studio: "It may have something of gloom about it and that was my intention in painting it – Though a cave may be a gloomy object in Nature – a view of its entrance gives rise to those trains of pensive feeling and thought that I have always found the most exquisitely delightful."[8] Perhaps the cave even helped inspire the creation of the sequel for *The Garden*, a painting Cole was hurrying to complete in time for the National Academy exhibition in May 1828. On April 11, Cole had written to Wadsworth about his plans to finish "a companion picture to the Garden of Eden – *The Expulsion of our first Parents from Eden.*" In the *Expulsion* (pl. 2), Cole faithfully replicated a portion of *The Garden*, including the cave. However, he greatly enlarged and moved the cave to the center of the *Expulsion*, where it became the gate separating Eden from the fallen world.[9]

Examination of the painting through x-radiography not only clarified the location and relative size of the drying cracks in *The Garden* but also provided additional information about the condition of support, ground, and paint layers. There were no tears in the original canvas, but the tacking edges had been removed during relining and the painting had been remounted on the present, slightly larger stretcher. This had relatively little impact on the visual integrity of the image, which, when compared to the Smillie engraving, is virtually complete. The scalloping of canvas threads on all four edges from the initial stretching of the canvas, also visible in the x-radiograph, confirmed that the painting had never been cut or enlarged.

The x-radiograph also confirmed that relatively little original paint had been lost through flaking; in addition to predictable losses along the edges and the nine small losses in the upper right quadrant, two minor losses appeared in the lower center and lower left corner of the picture. It also established that Cole's original paint layers in the cave area, which had contracted into islands, probably were largely intact beneath subsequent layers of restoration.

Examination under ultraviolet light revealed that there were no recently applied retouches and suggested that any damages or retouches were already visible to the naked eye. There were no indications of cleaning tests; the thick, aged varnish layers fluoresced a strong milky green, typical of a discolored natural resin varnish.

Infrared reflectography revealed faint indications of preliminary underdrawing in the landscape. Cole outlined the right side of the mountain, precisely replicating the contours of Mount Chocorua – which Cole had seen on a summer sketching trip to the White Mountains of New Hampshire in 1827 – and he may have outlined some of the other landmasses as well. However, there was no evidence of either the freehand sketching or the diagrammatical underdrawing sometimes detected in his later work,[10] although additional underdrawing may be concealed by opaque paint layers that prevent detection with the infrared vidicon system.

Cole's account books provide only a little information on the source and nature of the materials he used for painting but indicate an early interest in fine materials and, in particular, quality frames. He purchased one stretcher and canvas from Parker & Clover in New York in 1829, and may have secured canvas from Thomas Lynch, New York, and pigments and varnish from Feuchtwhanger.[11]

Parker & Clover, New York gilders and frame and looking-glass manufacturers, supplied Cole with twenty-eight frames as well as stretchers and a palette between 1827 and 1833.[12]

They were the source for the original frames for *The Garden* and the *Expulsion*, each of which cost forty dollars. Parker & Clover's original invoice to Thomas Cole from the period from 1827 to August 21, 1833, contains the following entry on June 26, 1828:[13]

June 26	1 (Picture Frame) Eden	$40.00
	1 (Picture Frame) Expulsion	$40.00

This was substantially more than the price of the frame Cole ordered for "*The Last of the Mohicans*" (Wadsworth Atheneum, Hartford, Connecticut) for Daniel Wadsworth: Cole noted in his November 26, 1827, letter to his patron that "The frame cost $15.00."[14] Considering that the Eden landscapes subsequently sold for four hundred dollars each, this was a considerable investment for the young artist painting the two works on speculation. Cole evidently had a keen interest in frames and understood their visual impact on paintings. His correspondence with his patrons Daniel Wadsworth and Robert Gilmor contains many references to frames, his selection of them, their prices, and characteristics. In his letter of November 26, 1827, Cole discussed a frame he had selected for Wadsworth's "*Last of the Mohicans*": "perhaps I have gone too high a price. . . . There is a good deal of ornament about it – it is better for the picture on that account as it reflects much light upon it."[15] In a letter to Gilmor, Cole wrote, "The Garden etc. are very handsomely framed."[16] And Cole wrote to Wadsworth, "My large pictures of Eden have been a great loss to me in time and money, the frames were expensive."[17]

The original frame for *The Garden* is currently unlocated. After its acquisition by the Amon Carter Museum, the painting was placed in an early nineteenth-century American frame similar to frames that would have been available to the artist in New York or Boston. The frame on the *Expulsion*, however, appears to be original.[18] Like the frame for "*The Last of the Mohicans*," it has an ogee profile. It is gilded with bold composition ornament, employing shell and floral motifs, applied to the corners and centers of each side. The outer edges of the frame contain fine egg-and-dart carving, while a gold liner with a rough, sandy texture surrounds the picture itself.[19]

There is no specific documentation about the source of painting materials Cole used in creating *The Garden*, but some observations about his materials can be made by examining the x-radiograph. Cole utilized a plain weave canvas, which he presumably primed himself, using a white lead ground. The artist apparently spread the ground with a spatula or palette knife in an arc-like pattern, with strokes running diagonally from the lower left to the upper right. Cole's use of a palette knife to apply the ground in *The Garden* represented a technical advance from his earlier use of a wide brush in works such as *Lake with Dead Trees* of 1825 (Allen Memorial Art Museum, Oberlin College, Oberlin, Ohio) and *Landscape, the Seat of Mr. Featherstonagh in the Distance* (location unknown) and *The Falls of Kaaterskill* (Warner Collection of Gulf States Paper Corporation, Tuscaloosa, Alabama) of 1826. In these earlier works the rough texture of brushstrokes in the ground remains visible in the upper paint layers and produces a surface much cruder in character than the smoother, refined one in *The Garden*. The use of the palette knife may also have allowed Cole to keep the ground layer relatively thin as well as even.

Figure 49. Thomas Cole, *Study of Clouds*, oil on canvas, 1846–47, 48 x 72 in., Philadelphia Museum of Art, on loan from Mr. and Mrs. John Merriam

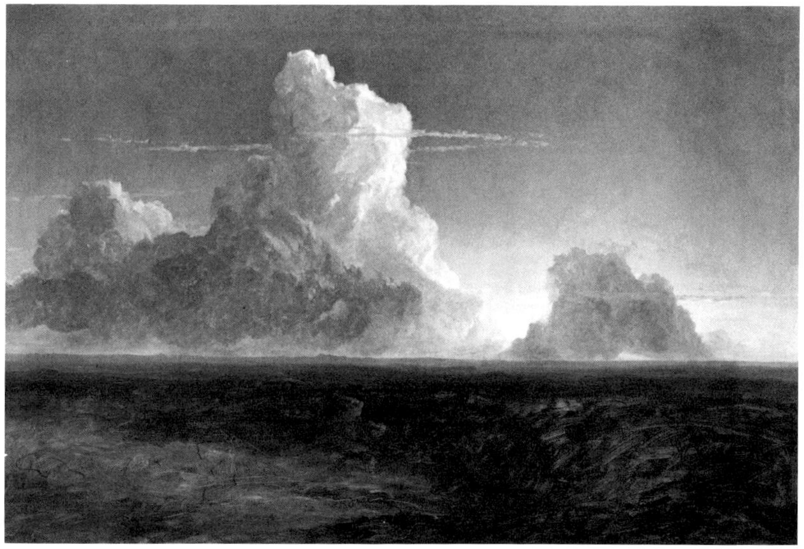

Next he blocked in the major outlines of the composition in the middle distance, such as the copse of trees on the left, the hills and waterfall, and the large tree on the right. These outlines replicate, in reverse, the basic compositional outlines of John Martin's *Paphian Bower* of 1826, a mezzotint of which was widely available in New York (see Kelly, fig. 33) and a summary sketch of which survives among Cole's drawings.[20] The similarity between Martin's composition and Cole's is perhaps more striking in the x-radiograph of *The Garden* than in the painting itself. The x-radiograph records Cole's initial conception of the large tree on the right with open, forked branches similar to the tree that frames the left side of Martin's *Paphian Bower.* Cole then laid in the sky, later adding details such as branches, palm fronds, the vine, and perhaps even the mountain. As previously noted, he used preliminary underdrawing to outline the crisp contour of the mountain – one of the principal elements in the composition – and fine underdrawing for some of the surrounding terrain and followed these contours faithfully as he painted the mountains. In other parts of the landscape, however, Cole reworked areas or made adjustments as he developed the composition. He shifted the tree at right slightly to the left and made its trunk thicker. After establishing the major elements in the composition, Cole last turned his attention to the foreground, the area with the most intricate and extensive detail.

In the unfinished *Expulsion – Moon and Firelight* (pl. 3), painted about the same year as *The Garden* as a part of the same series, Cole's working method remains more visible, suggesting the process by which he derived the Museum's picture. Cole first completed the principal elements in the center of the composition – the bridge and the cave – after boldly blocking in peripheral elements. The liveliness of this initial brushwork is often erased in his subsequent reworking and finishing of the surface. In his first laying in of the composition, brushwork follows form, as in the gnarled trees in the lower left or the rocks in the right of the unfinished *Expulsion*.

This followed what seems to have been his frequent practice, because three unfinished late works – *Study of Clouds* (1846–47; fig. 49), *Cross at Sunset* (1847, Thyssen-Bornemisza Collection, Madrid, Spain), and *Gothic Ruins at Sunset* (c. 1847, Kennedy Galleries, New York) – indicate a blocking in of the main elements of the landscape with vigorous brushwork. In these late works, the foreground was the last area Cole addressed, and he utilized a variety of drawing techniques, including graphite, brush, and sgrafitto, a method of scratching into the still-wet paint layers with the butt end of the brush to work out the placement of foreground details. He might have employed these techniques in *The Garden* as well, although these preliminary stages are no longer visible under the finished surface of the painting.

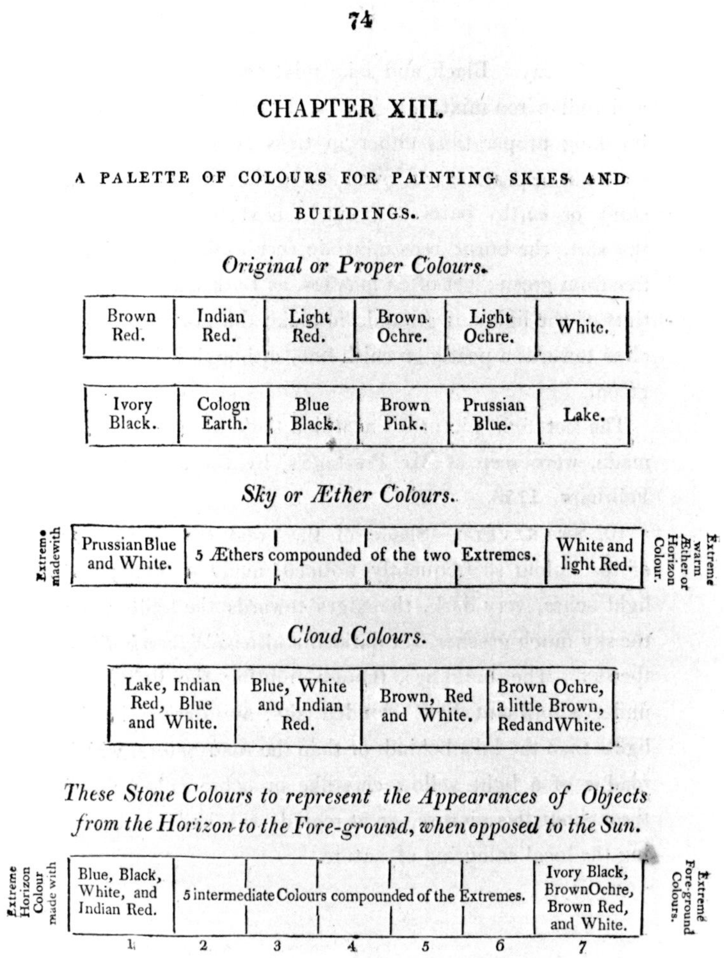
74

CHAPTER XIII.

A PALETTE OF COLOURS FOR PAINTING SKIES AND BUILDINGS.

Original or Proper Colours.

Brown Red.	Indian Red.	Light Red.	Brown Ochre.	Light Ochre.	White.
Ivory Black.	Cologn Earth.	Blue Black.	Brown Pink.	Prussian Blue.	Lake.

Sky or Æther Colours.

Extreme madewith	Prussian Blue and White.	5 Æthers compounded of the two Extremes.					White and light Red.	Extreme warm Æther or Horizon Colour.

Cloud Colours.

Lake, Indian Red, Blue and White.	Blue, White and Indian Red.	Brown, Red and White.	Brown Ochre, a little Brown, Red and White.

These Stone Colours to represent the Appearances of Objects from the Horizon to the Fore-ground, when opposed to the Sun.

Extreme Horizon Colour made with	Blue, Black, White, and Indian Red.	5 intermediate Colours compounded of the Extremes.					Ivory Black, Brown Ochre, Brown Red, and White.	Extreme Fore-ground Colours.
	1	2	3	4	5	6	7	

Figure 50. "A Palette of Colours for Painting Skies and Buildings," page from Oram's *Treatise*

In *The Garden* as in the two *Expulsion* paintings, Cole worked from a generalized, free sketching-in of major elements to a final, highly finished paint surface embroidered with details so intricate that some can only be appreciated upon close inspection. This is particularly true of the lake area in the central foreground, surrounded by sunlit trees and palms, which Cole sometimes embellished with tiny dashes or dots of pale yellow; the pair of miniature elephants marching to the left; and the delicate palms that punctuate the distant island and coastline.

The refinement of Cole's paint handling in *The Garden* represents a dramatic leap forward from his first landscapes upon his arrival in New York. This was a period in which Cole was rapidly maturing as an artist. Although by his own admission, he "had never seen a fine picture by any foreign landscape painter," he regularly referred to works by Claude Lorrain, Richard Wilson, and Salvator Rosa in correspondence with his patrons.[21] Earlier, when Cole worked as a teacher of drawing and painting in Steubenville, Ohio, the portrait painter Stein gave him "an English work on painting." The book dealt with composition, color, and design and was illustrated with engravings. Cole studied the book assiduously, and it clearly fed his ambition to become a great painter.[22] He would later write that the book was his "companion day and night."[23] By the time of his arrival in New York, he was carefully studying techniques described in another painting treatise, *Precepts and Observations on the Art of Colouring in Landscape Painting by the late William Oram, Esq.* (London, 1810), and copying passages into a notebook.[24] Oram's treatise was illustrated with engraved plates after the author's landscape designs, containing written notations of variations of light and color; it also had chapters on painting skies, clouds, and foliage, and described paint mixtures and formulas for specific landscape effects. The treatise also dealt with the initial laying in of a composition and methods for achieving effects of light and aerial perspective in landscapes. It even provided "a palette of colours for painting skies and buildings" (fig. 50).

Oram also included numerous "observations on the colouring of several Eminent Masters," notably Nicolas Poussin, Domenichino, Gaspar Poussin, Van der Neer, and Wouvermans. In fact, Cole hoped that the sale of *The Garden* would fund an extended trip to Europe, where he could continue his artistic education, study the works of these old master painters firsthand, and meet the leading English landscape painters of the day.

After his arrival in New York in 1825, Cole transcribed extracts from *The Art of Colouring in Landscape Painting* in a notebook, including notes on painting skies and foliage. Oram's notes may have proved particularly useful for Cole in his efforts to create an ideal landscape. The artist noted Oram's formula for painting a misty morning sky:

> A misty Morning when the sun is about an hour high and the fogs are partly cleared the sky on and about the horizon is very light to be made with white a very small portion of blue a touch a light red or perhaps only ochre. as we look higher there is more blue added but very tenderly mingled and not even the higher part of the sky is a strong blue.[25]

In creating the distant mountains in *The Garden*, however, Cole departed from Oram's treatise, painting them not "the colour of the higher part of the sky" but a pale lavender. Following Oram's suggestion, however, he painted the nearer mountains darker and the more distant ones paler (pl. 4).

Cole's treatment of the foliage in *The Garden* also seems consistent with Oram's treatise. From chapter 7 Cole wrote: "when the sun shines on the bough the extreme heightenings are much yellower and lighter than the mezzotinto lights and here and there a little very bright touching somewhat pale is found in the extreme lights." Cole's handling of bright yellow highlights on the sunlit foliage in the upper left and to the left of the cave follows this formula (pl. 5).

In creating the dark swamp area (pl. 6), Cole may have followed Oram's suggestions for portraying foliage in shadow: "The lights of the boughs in soft shade are of a slatish cool colour very little green marked off or interspersed with a darker colour rather more green and some think blacker and thus proceeding til it comes into the darkest colour of all in which there is not the least appearance of green."

On the left of *The Garden*, Cole shaped the tree forms with thin, dark washes of green pigment. He then added layers of carefully observed foliage, in which he described the individual forms of leaves, fruit, flowers, birds, and vines. One of the most beautifully preserved passages is in the lower left, where a richly colored bird perches above a garden of tropical flowers with butterflies resting (pl. 7). Cole used his most intense colors to depict foreground details, "brilliant marble, golden sands, pebbles of every dye – banks of beauteous flowers, fruits"[26] – with brilliant red, blue, yellow, pink, and orange. These were created with a very fine brush, loaded with pigment. He developed crisp highlights and shadows and elements such as petals or butterflies' wings with numerous added strokes of unblended color, sometimes painting wet-in-wet (pl. 8). Most of the foreground is built up through layering opaque, unblended brushstrokes over thinner washes of color. Cole's general working method involves achieving the effects with direct applications of opaque paint to the ground or underlayers, rather than through a sophisticated use of layering the paint with glazes or scumbles. Cole's painting emphasized brushwork; however, it is not immediate or spontaneous but is carefully controlled. It aimed to create accurately illusionistic effects and to record details of flora and fauna in a landscape.

The tonality of the sky in *The Garden* ranges from a more intense sky blue in the upper left, where the pale crescent moon seems to sink behind the trees, to a paler, almost cream-colored vapor to the right, where the sun is rising. The mountains and clouds are painted with pale yellows and lavenders; warmer, luminous yellow dabs of color appear on the foliage in the middle foreground. The view of Mount Chocorua is framed by foliage (pl. 4), and these areas as well as the foreground are predominantly shades of dark greens with dark gray-green shadows and warm yellow highlights. The hillock on which Adam and Eve stand is bathed in sunlight and appears a paler yellow green. Cole may have added pale yellow glazes to clouds, waterfalls, reflections on the lake, and to the lower part of sky.

In the companion piece showing the *Expulsion from the Garden of Eden*, Cole achieved a thickly painted, enamel-like surface with dramatic contrasts of light and shade. He created the dark and menacing tonality by painting the darker passages very directly with almost monochromatic glazes of brown and black pigments, using sulphurous orange highlights to pick out details. Cole titled the diagrammatic sketch for this painting "Scale of Colour for the Expulsion" (see also Kelly, fig. 29). This drawing indicates the chromatic sequence that Cole wished to employ in the final painting. He used concentric circles that emanate from the brightest point in the composition – the cave – and the color notes in each band show a progression from light to dark tones and warm to cool colors. It is impossible to look at this sketch without recalling the chromatic diagrams illustrated in early nineteenth-century English treatises.[27]

Cole's treatment of the cooler sky and mountains in the upper right of the *Expulsion* is very similar to that in *The Garden*. Many of the details – flowers, rocks, and so on – seem directly lifted from the earlier composition. There is also a fine network of drying cracks throughout the foliage in the *Expulsion*, but these are less severe than in *The Garden*. Coincidentally, marked drying cracks also exist in the central cave area of the *Expulsion*, an element that had also created technical problems in *The Garden*.

The delicacy and variety of Cole's technique only became apparent as the treatment of the picture progressed in the spring of 1990. The paint film initially was consolidated with gelatin, which was selected for its compatibility with the painting's preexisting glue lining. It soon became clear that a stronger adhesive was needed to secure the lifting paint. The entire paint surface was eventually consolidated locally with dilute Beva in toluene.[28]

The painting was spit-cleaned to remove the thick layers of grime that had accumulated on the surface. Solvent cleaning proceeded, with the cleaning of the cave area being postponed until it could be assessed in relation to surrounding areas and compared with the Smillie engraving. The varnish layers – thick, brown with age, and opaque – were unveiled gradually, over several days, with dramatic results.

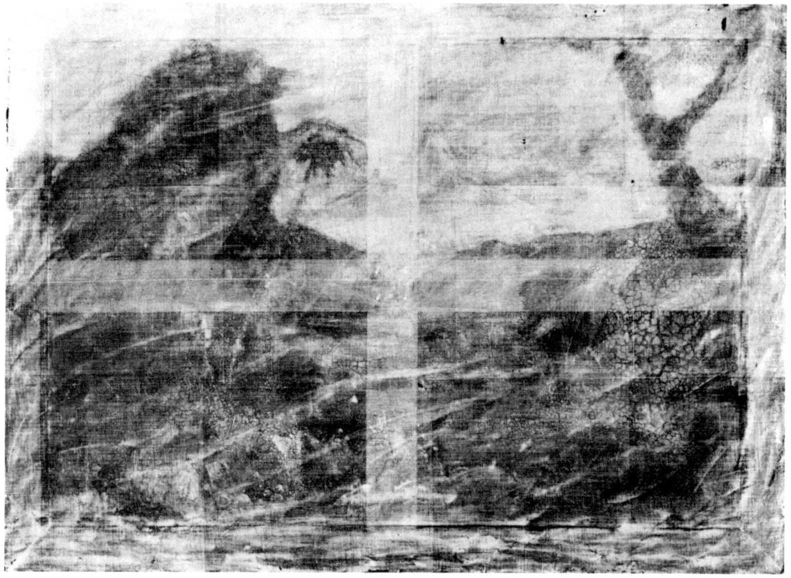

Figure 51. X-radiograph of *The Garden of Eden*, 1990

It is unlikely that Cole's original varnish remained on *The Garden*. Although Cole referred often to varnishing in letters to his patrons, he never directly identified the nature of his varnish in this period. However, he may have used copal as the varnish for *The Garden*. In a letter to the painter Asher B. Durand in 1836, Cole asked: "Will you please obtain for me a pint of Copal Varnish from Feughtwhangher [*sic*] if he now has any very fine."[29] Copal varnish, made from a variety of hard resins,[30] causes cracks when applied over soft coats of paint. And although copal varnishes were admired for the quality of their blended, smooth surfaces, they turned very yellow and even brown upon aging.[31]

Numerous subtle details emerged in the cleaning that had been obscured previously: a pale crescent-shaped moon became visible in the upper left, as did delicately painted pairs of birds in flight, butterflies on flowers, and in the distance, elephants in a sunlit meadow (pl. 9). Removing the discolored varnish, which obscured the illusion of depth, clarified relationships among forms in space. This was particularly evident on the right side, where the volume of the trunk and branches of the great tree emerged, and on the left, where the trees and swamp could be read.

Every effort was made during cleaning to maintain the proper balance between the luminous light areas in the middle ground and distance and the darker areas of the landscape, particularly the gloomy swamp on the left and the shadowy cave on the right. The light areas, which were painted with white lead, have changed relatively little because this pigment is very stable, but the darker areas have undergone a significant transformation. In addition to developing the aforementioned drying cracks, these passages were thinly painted and appear to have grown darker and more transparent with age.[32]

Cleaning tests in the cave area, performed under the microscope, revealed that elements of Cole's original composition existed beneath the overpaint. Traces of the cascade that flowed from the cave's mouth, red branches, parts of rocks, and the dark silhouettes of fir trees were identified, all consistent with the elements in Smillie's engraving. Removing the overpaint and varnish exposed the wide drying cracks seen in the x-radiograph of this area (fig. 51). At this point, the light colors that Cole had used in his initial rendition of the lake and hillside became apparent in the grayish cracks, producing a startling contrast with the islands of darker pigment that remained from the layer he applied on top of this earlier compositional element.

After cleaning, the painting was varnished with a brush coat of damar. Flake losses were filled with gesso and inpainted with watercolors and pigments in varnish; drying cracks were also inpainted. There was some reconstruction in the cave area, rock, cypress tree, and traveller's palm, using Smillie's engraving as a guide, and the wide drying cracks in the cave were filled and inpainted. However, the area continued to present a textural problem which was distracting even after inpainting was completed: the wrinkled islands of original paint in the cave area appeared matte, and the inpainted drying cracks, smooth and glossy. These textural differences were alleviated by applying a colorless gel medium to the cracks, which helped reduce gloss and create an even surface. This area was further integrated with additional spray coats of damar varnish.

The recent restoration of *The Garden of Eden* by Thomas Cole provided the challenge of cleaning and retouching the most important imaginary landscape of the artist's early career, and one that had not yet been seen by modern scholars. *The Garden* was created during Cole's first years in New York, a period in which he felt that he was working diligently toward "the attainment of excellence in my art,"[33] studying engravings after the old masters, reading Oram's treatise on coloring in landscape painting, and discussing his work frequently with his patrons. In spite of his efforts, however, Cole in writing to Wadsworth about *The Garden of Eden* in November 1828 was clearly dejected over the still unsold painting: "I have not yet disposed of my Garden – *there* was a loss of between three or four months in the last year." As he had stated earlier in the letter, he had hoped to finance a trip to Europe from the sale of the painting: "it is not the riches I aspire to. . . . I long to see the works of the Great Masters and to profit by them."[34]

The problems that resulted from his still imperfect technique and his reworking of a significant area of the composition have compromised certain aspects of the painting we see today. Nevertheless, these problems have not diminished Cole's achievements in *The Garden* or the lyrical poetry evident throughout. In the great works of his maturity – *The Course of Empire* and *The Voyage of Life* – Cole seems to have overcome many of the technical shortcomings evident in *The Garden*; however, he seldom surpasses its magical atmosphere. Although he himself felt at its conception that the beauty he wished to create was more "than my art can realize," *The Garden of Eden* surely conveys much of what Cole considered the "heavenly atmosphere in the pictures of the imagination."[35]

CLAIRE M. BARRY

Acknowledgments

I would like to thank Jan Muhlert for the wonderful opportunity to restore The Garden of Eden *and for her constant support and advice throughout this project. I am also greatly indebted to Edmund Pillsbury and the Kimbell Art Foundation for graciously allowing the restoration to be carried out in the conservation studio of the Kimbell Art Museum in the spring of 1990. I would like to thank Doreen Bolger for her important contribution to the restoration of* The Garden of Eden *as well as for her invaluable advice during the development of this essay. I am also deeply grateful to Sarah Cash and Michael Gallagher for reviewing this text and for their insightful comments and suggestions. My thanks also go to Milan R. Hughston for his bibliographic assistance throughout my work on* The Garden of Eden, *and Eleanor Jones and Lee Parry for answering my lingering questions. Finally, I am grateful to Carol Clark and Charles Parkhurst for reviewing the final draft.*

NOTES

1. Quoted in Ellwood C. Parry III, *The Art of Thomas Cole: Ambition and Imagination* (Newark: University of Delaware Press, 1988), p. 70. See also Franklin Kelly's essay in this catalogue on Cole's conception of *The Garden of Eden*, "A Higher Style of Landscape," pp. 21–29.

2. James Smillie (1807–1855) was born in Edinburgh, Scotland, and settled in New York in 1830 as a banknote engraver. He engraved on steel the works of some of the leading American painters of the early to mid-nineteenth century. He was especially successful as an engraver of landscapes and was an associate member of the National Academy of Design (1832–51). Smillie created several prints after Thomas Cole's paintings, including *The Garden of Eden* in 1831–32, when it was in the possession of Charles Wilkes. Smillie's engraving of *The Garden* was reproduced as the frontispiece for volume one of the Holy Bible, published by Gray and Bowen in Boston in 1831 and now extremely rare. Smillie also made four large prints after Cole's allegorical series *The Voyage of Life*, one of the finest and most ambitious engraving projects undertaken in the United States in the 1850s.

3. For a discussion of the effects of contraction, see Sheldon Keck, "Mechanical Alteration of the Paint Film," *Studies in Conservation: The Journal of the International Institute for Conservation of Historic and Artistic Works* 14, no. 1 (February 1969): 16. In oil or oil-resin paints these premature cracks are largely the result of inherent vice, involving defective paint formulation or faulty and untimely application. Since oil paint may remain plastic or thermoplastic for long periods of time, the formation of these drying cracks may begin within weeks after paint application, but in some cases may continue for fifty years or longer.

4. Cole may have varnished his paintings too soon after they were completed. The use of copal varnish in particular would exacerbate this problem. Applying the hard resin varnish too soon over a soft paint film would cause cracks. In general, the longer a picture has to dry, the better. As Cole wrote to Wadsworth on June 5, 1828, shortly after he completed *View of L'Esperance on the Schoharie River,* "it wants varnish – but it will be well to leave it one month longer"; quoted in J. Bard McNulty, ed., *The Correspondence of Thomas Cole and Daniel Wadsworth* (Hartford: The Connecticut Historical Society, 1983), p. 42.

5. R. H. Marijnissen, *Paintings: Genuine Fraud Fake: Modern Methods of Examining Paintings* (Brussels: Librico, 1985), p. 115. Drying craquelure can form from an excess of binder; the rapid contraction of binder upon drying; from the use of pigments such as ivory black or emerald green, which require a great deal of binder owing to their fine grains; from the use of resinous paint media; or from overpainting layers not yet dry to the touch or applying the varnish layer too early.

6. Marijnissen, *Paintings*, p. 115.

7. Cole to Wadsworth, November 26, 1827; quoted in McNulty, *Correspondence*, p. 20.

8. Cole to Wadsworth, April 23, 1828; quoted in McNulty, *Correspondence*, p. 38.

9. For a discussion on the role of the cave in the *Expulsion*, see Ellen Avitts Meneffe, "The Early Biblical Landscapes of Thomas Cole (1825–1829)," Ph.D. diss., Rice University, 1987, pp. 40–41.

10. See Dan A. Kushel, "Some Observations on Thomas Cole's *Voyage of Life* Using Infrared Reflectography and X-radiography," in Paul D. Schweizer, ed., *The Voyage of Life by Thomas Cole: Paintings, Drawings, and Prints* (Utica, N.Y.: Museum of Art, Munson-Williams-Proctor Institute, 1985), p. 54.

11. Alexander W. Katlan, *American Artists' Materials, vol. 2, A Guide to Stretchers, Panels, Millboards, and Stencil Marks*, ed. Peter Hastings Falk, 2 vols. (Madison, Conn.: Sound View Press, 1992), 2:497.

12. Katlan, *American Artists' Materials*, 2:495.

13. Parker & Clover, invoice to Thomas Cole, April 14, 1827-May 13, 1833, quoted in Katlan, *American Artists' Materials*, 2:499.

14. Cole to Wadsworth, November 26, 1827; quoted in McNulty, *Correspondence*, p. 21.

15. Ibid.

16. Cole to Gilmor, January 5, 1829; quoted in Howard S. Merritt, ed., "Correspondence between Thomas Cole and Robert Gilmor, Jr.," in *Studies on Thomas Cole, an American Romanticist* (Maryland: The Baltimore Museum of Art, 1967), p. 60.

17. Cole to Gilmor, January 20, 1829; quoted in Merritt, "Correspondence," p. 62.

18. See David Steinberg's observation that the frame on the *Expulsion* and that for "*The Last of the Mohicans*" were probably made by Parker & Clover, New York. McNulty, *Correspondence*, p. 23. Also, Andy Haines, Exhibitions Preparator for the Paintings Department at the Museum of Fine Arts, Boston, believes the frame on the *Expulsion* is likely to be original.

19. William Adair, *The Frame in America, 1700–1900: A Survey of Fabrication Techniques and Styles* (Washington, D.C.: The American Institute of Architects Foundation, 1983), pp. 29–30.

20. See Kelly, "A Higher Style of Landscape," pp. 38–39.

21. Cole to Gilmor, January 2, 1827; quoted in Merritt, "Correspondence," p. 50.

22. For a discussion of Cole's years in Steubenville, Ohio, the importance of the English treatise, and his relationship with John Stein, see also Alan Wallach, "Thomas Cole: Landscape and the Course of American Empire," in *Thomas Cole: Landscape into History,* ed. by William H. Truettner and Alan Wallach (New Haven and London: Yale University Press, and Washington, D.C.: National Museum of American Art, 1994), p. 25.

23. Ibid., quoting William Dunlap, *History of the Rise and Progress of the Arts of Design in the United States* (1834; reprint, New York: Dover Publications, 1969), 2:352.

24. Wallach, "Thomas Cole," p. 28, and Thomas Cole, extracts transcribed from William Oram, *Precepts and Observations on the Art of Colouring in Landscape Painting,* in a notebook dated 1825 in the collection of the Detroit Institute of Arts (39.681 [formerly 39.558B]).

25. Ibid.

26. Cole to Wadsworth, November 26, 1827; quoted in McNulty, *Correspondence,* p. 20.

27. See also William I. Homer, "Thomas Cole and Field's 'Chromatography,'" *Princeton Museum Record* 19 (1960): 26–30, for a discussion on Cole's interest in Field's color diagrams and in the expressive power and harmony of colors. Cole wrote on November 8, 1834, about making a small circular diagram of colors. It is difficult to know when the artist first became aware of Field's writings. Field's first book on the subject, *Chromatics, or an Essay on the Analogy and Harmony of Colours,* was published in London in 1817, and his *Chromatography or a Treatise on Colours and Pigments,* which included the color diagram as its frontispiece, was published in London in 1835. I would like to thank Ellwood C. Parry III for pointing out that Cole also painted a Diagram of Contrasts in oil on panel, 25 x 35 inches, c. 1834 (Collection of Mrs. Barbara Johnson, Princeton, New Jersey). It is reproduced in Mary Black's *What Is American About American Art?* (New York: M. Knoedler & Co., Inc., 1971), p. 53.

28. Robert L. Feller, Nathan Stolow, and Elizabeth H. Jones, *On Picture Varnishes and Their Solvents* (Cleveland: The Press of Case Western Reserve University, 1971), p. 175.

29. Cole to Durand, May 24, 1836, in Thomas Cole Papers, New York State Library, Albany; quoted in Katlan, *American Artists' Materials,* 1:19; 2:497.

30. Rutherford J. Gettens and George Stout, eds., *Painting Materials: A Short Encyclopedia* (New York: Dover, 1966), p. 15. Fossil resin is the hardest and most widely used resin in copal varnish.

31. Max Doerner, *The Materials of the Artist* (New York: Harcourt, Brace and World), p. 158.

32. Marijnissen, *Paintings,* p. 119: "As an oil dries its refractive index increases. In practice this means that the paint layer becomes increasingly transparent with age."

33. Cole to Wadsworth, November 10, 1828; quoted in McNulty, *Correspondence,* p. 47.

34. Cole to Wadsworth, November 10, 1828; quoted in McNulty, *Correspondence,* p. 49.

35. Cole to Wadsworth, November 10, 1828; quoted in McNulty, *Correspondence,* p. 47.

Thomas Cole's Paintings of Eden *Amon Carter Museum (February 18 – May 28, 1995)*

[*All works by Thomas Cole (1801–1848) unless otherwise noted*]

The Garden of Eden *and Related Works*

The Garden of Eden, oil on canvas, 1828, 38½ x 52¾ in., Amon Carter Museum, 1990.10 [pl. 1]

Chocorua Peak, New Hampshire, pen and black ink over pencil, c. 1827, 7⅞ x 12¼ in., Detroit Institute of Arts, Founders Society Purchase, William H. Murphy Fund, 39.182 [fig. 8]

Study for *The Garden of Eden*, pencil, 1827/28, 7½ x 12¾ in., Detroit Institute of Arts, Founders Society Purchase, William H. Murphy Fund, 39.300A [fig. 14]

Study for *The Garden of Eden*, pen and black ink over pencil, 1827/28, 10 x 15⁵⁄₁₆ in., Detroit Institute of Arts, Founders Society Purchase, William H. Murphy Fund, 39.357 [fig. 15]

John Martin (1789–1854), *Adam and Eve – The Morning Hymn*, mezzotint in John Milton's *Paradise Lost*, 1827, plate: 7¾ x 10¾ in., image: 5¹¹⁄₁₆ x 8⅛ in., National Gallery of Art, 1979.68.1 [fig. 7]

George Henry Phillips (w. 1819–1852), after John Martin (1789–1854), *The Paphian Bower*, mezzotint, 1826, plate: 19⁵⁄₁₆ x 25⅝ in., sheet: 20⅝ x 26¾ in., The Metropolitan Museum of Art, 67.797.45(a) [fig. 33]

James Smillie (1807–1855), after Thomas Cole (1801–1848), *The Garden of Eden*, engraving, 1831–32, 4½ x 6 in., frontispiece for vol. 1 of the Holy Bible published by Gray and Bowen (Boston, 1831), New York Public Library, Astor, Lenox and Tilden Foundations [fig. 36]

Expulsion – Moon and Firelight *and Related Works*

The Expulsion–Moon and Firelight, oil on canvas, c. 1827/28, 36 x 48¹⁄₁₆ in., Thyssen-Bornemisza Collection, 1980.14 [pl. 3]

The Bridge of Fear, pencil, 1827/28, sheet: 9¼ x 7½ in., image: 5¾ x 4⅞ in., Detroit Institute of Arts, Founders Society Purchase, William H. Murphy Fund, 39.367 [fig. 24]

The Bridge of Fear, pencil and black crayon with gray wash, 1827/28, 9³⁄₁₆ x 7³⁄₁₆ in., National Gallery of Art, John Davis Hatch Collection, 1979.20.17 [fig. 25]

The Bridge of Fear, pencil, 1827, 7⅞ x 9⁷⁄₁₆ in., Detroit Institute of Arts, Founders Society Purchase, William H. Murphy Fund, 39.219A [fig. 23]

Expulsion from the Garden of Eden *and Related Works*

Expulsion from the Garden of Eden, oil on canvas, 1828, 39 x 54 in., Museum of Fine Arts, Boston, 47.1188 [pl. 2]

Sketchbook, begun in 1827, each sheet $9\frac{5}{8}$ x $7\frac{3}{16}$ in., New York State Library, Albany, Manuscripts Division, DJ10635; sketchbook pages 1, 13, 27, 20, 17, 13, 32, 40, 27, 28, 79, 75, 67, 68, and 19 [reproduced as figs. 4, 9, 10, 12, 16, 17, 18, 19, 20, 21, 26, 27, 28, 29, and 35, respectively]

Study for *Expulsion from the Garden of Eden*, pencil, probably 1828, $9\frac{13}{16}$ x $15\frac{5}{8}$ in., Detroit Institute of Arts, Founders Society Purchase, William H. Murphy Fund, 39.294A [fig. 30]

Study for *Expulsion from the Garden of Eden*, pen and black ink, wash, and pencil, 1828, $13\frac{13}{16}$ x $19\frac{5}{16}$ in., Detroit Institute of Arts, Founders Society Purchase, William H. Murphy Fund, 39.483A [fig. 31]

Study for *Expulsion from the Garden of Eden*, pen, pencil, and wash, 1828, 11 x $16\frac{1}{2}$ in., Detroit Institute of Arts, Founders Society Purchase, William H. Murphy Fund, 39.366B [fig. 32]

John Martin (1789-1854), *Adam and Eve Driven Out of Paradise*, mezzotint proof from John Milton's *Paradise Lost*, 1827, $13\frac{7}{8}$ x 10 in., Museum of Fine Arts, Boston, 69.1326 [fig. 34]

Bibliography for *The Garden of Eden*

Exhibitions:

Annual Exhibition, National Academy of Design, New York, May 5–July 10, 1828, no. 24; Private exhibition, Old Athenaeum, Boston, August–December 1828; Elam Bliss Bookstore, New York, May 1829; Review Exhibition, National Academy of Design, New York, May–June 25, 1831, no. 50

Literature:

1828 "National Academy of Arts and Design." *New-York Mirror* 5 (May 24), p. 367.

1828 *New-York Morning Courier* (June 21), p. 2. Quoted in Christopher Kent Wilson, "Rediscovered Thomas Cole Letter: New Light on the *Expulsion from the Garden of Eden*," *American Art Journal* 18 (Winter 1986): 73–74.

1828 *American* 9 (June 23), p. 2. Quoted in Wilson, "Rediscovered Cole Letter."

1828 *New-York Morning Courier* (June 24), p. 2. Quoted in Wilson, "Rediscovered Cole Letter."

1828 *Boston Recorder and Religious Telegraph* 13 (August 22): 135.

1829 *Commercial Advertiser* (April 16), unconfirmed

1829 *New-York Evening Post* (May 15), p. 2.

1829 *New-York Evening Post* (May 21), p. 2.

1829 "Cole's Paradise." *New-York Morning Courier* 5 (May 22), p. 2.

1831 *New York Evening Post* (May 7), p. 2.

1831 "The Fine Arts: National Academy of Design." *New-York Mirror* 8 (May 7), p. 350.

1843 Lanman, Charles. "Cole's Imaginative Paintings." *The United States Magazine and DemocraticReview* 12 (June): 599.

1848 Bryant, William Cullen. *A Funeral Oration Occasioned by the Death of Thomas Cole, Delivered Before the National Academy of Design, New York, May 4, 1848.* New York: D. Appleton & Co., pp. 28–29.

1853 Noble, Louis Legrand. *Course of Empire. Voyage of Life and other Pictures.* New York: Cornish, Lamport, & Co., pp. 91–92, 94–95, and 103.

1853 Review of *The Voyage of Life, Course of Empire, and Other Pictures of Thomas Cole*, etc., by Louis L. Noble. *North American Review* 161 (October 1853): 317.

1854 "Thomas Cole." *The National Magazine* 4 (April): 317, 320.

1855 Lewis, E. Anna. "Art and Artists of America: Thomas Cole." *Graham's Magazine* 46 (April): 336.

1859 Ripley, George, and Charles Dana, eds. *The New American Cyclopaedia*. New York: D. Appleton and Co., 5:459.

1860 "The Artists of America." *The Crayon* 7 (February): 46.

1860 Greene, George Washington. *Biographical Studies.* New York: G. P. Putnam, pp. 95–96.

1867 Tuckerman, Henry. *Book of the Artists*. New York: Putnam, pp. 230, 624.

1916 Hale, Edward E. "The Early Art of Thomas Cole." *Art in America* 4: 37, 39.

1934 Mather, Frank, Jr. "The Hudson River School." *The American Magazine of Art* 27 (June 1934): 302.

1948 *Thomas Cole 1801–1848 One Hundred Years Later*. Hartford, Conn.: Wadsworth Atheneum, pp. 6, 40–41, 50–51, and 57.

1949 *The M. and M. Karolik Collection of American Paintings 1815–1865*. Cambridge, Mass.: Harvard University Press, pp. 192, 194.

1954 La Budde, Kenneth James. "The Mind of Thomas Cole." Ph.D. diss., University of Minnesota, pp.74, 187–188, 210.

1957 Deutsch, Barbara Novak. "Cole and Durand: Criticism and Patronage (A Study of American Taste in Landscape, 1825–1865)." Ph. D.diss., Radcliffe College, pp. 130, 135–136, and 189.

1964 *An Exhibition of Paintings by Thomas Cole N. A. from the Artist's Studio, Catskill, New York*. NewYork: Kennedy Galleries, Inc., p. 18.

1964 Noble, Louis Legrand. *The Life and Works of Thomas Cole*. Edited by Eliot S. Vesell. Cambridge,Mass.: Harvard University Press, The Belknap Press, pp. 61–62, 64, 71–72, 316.

1967 *Studies on Thomas Cole, An American Romanticist*, Annual II. Baltimore: Baltimore Museum of Art, pp. 58, 59, 60–68, 84, 85, 86, 89, 105, 128.

1969 Hood, Graham. "Thomas Cole's Lost Hagar." *American Art Journal* 1 (Fall): 44.

1969 Merritt, Howard S. *Thomas Cole 1801–1848*. Rochester, New York: Memorial Art Gallery, University of Rochester, pp. 17, 25.

1970 Parry, Ellwood C., III. "Thomas Cole's *The Course of Empire*: A Study in Serial Imagery."Ph.D. diss., Yale University, pp. 14, 17, 19.

1973 Wallach, Alan Peter. "The Ideal American Artist and the Dissenting Tradition: A Study of Thomas Cole's Popular Reputation." Ph.D. diss., Columbia University, pp. 75, 80, 84, 151.

1978 Parry, Ellwood C., III. "Thomas Cole and the Practical Application of Landscape Theory." *New Mexico Studies in the Fine Arts* 3: 15–18, 21.

1979 Parry, Ellwood C., III. "Acts of God, Acts of Man: Geological Ideas and the Imaginary Landscapes of Thomas Cole," in *Two Hundred Years of Geology in America. Proceedings of the New Hampshire Bicentennial Conference on the History of Geology*. Edited by Cecil J. Schneer. New Hampshire: University Press of New England, pp. 58, 64.

1980 *Next to Nature: Landscape Paintings from the National Academy of Design*. New York: Harper & Row Publishers and National Academy of Design, p. 32.

1981 Baigell, Matthew. *Thomas Cole*. New York: Watson Guptill, pp. 40, 81.

1981 Crean, Hugh R. "Agony's Crown Attained: Thomas Cole and the Double Work of Art." *Arts Magazine* 56 (November): 92 and 93.

1981 Wallach, Alan. "Thomas Cole and the Aristocracy." *Arts Magazine* 56 (November): 100, 101, 106.

1981 Parry, Ellwood C., III. "Recent Discoveries in the Art of Thomas Cole." *The Magazine Antiques* 120 (November): 1157.

1982 Merritt, Howard S. *To Walk with Nature: The Drawings of Thomas Cole*. Yonkers, New York: The Hudson River Museum, pp. 19, 20.

1982 *Thyssen-Bornemisza Collection of American Nineteenth Century Landscapes.* Houston: The Museum of Fine Arts, p. 36.

1983 Kelly, Franklin. "Myth, Allegory, and Science: Thomas Cole's Paintings of Mount Etna." *Arts in Virginia* 23: 5, 15.

1983 McNulty, J. Bard, ed. *The Correspondence of Thomas Cole and Daniel Wadsworth.* Hartford: Connecticut Historical Society, pp. 20, 33, 37, 38, 42, 46, 49, 54.

1984 Brichta, Vivian. "Portfolio: Thomas Cole and the American Frontier." *American History Illustrated* 19 (March): 29–30. (Erroneously stated as having been purchased by Robert Gilmor Jr. in 1829.)

1984 Manthorne, Katherine. "The Quest for a Tropical Paradise: Palm Trees as Fact and Symbol in Latin American Landscape Imagery, 1850–1875." *Art Journal* 44 (Winter): 377. (Smillie print reproduced, p. 376.)

1985 Gerdts, William H. "American Landscape Painting: Critical Judgements 1730–1845." *American Art Journal* 17 (Winter): 47, 58, and 59.

1986 Nygren, Edward J., with Bruce Robertson. *Views and Visions: American Landscape Before 1830.* Washington, D.C.: The Corcoran Gallery of Art, pp. 179–185.

1986 Wilson, Christopher Kent. "Rediscovered Thomas Cole Letter: New Light on the *Expulsion from the Garden of Eden.*" *American Art Journal* 18: 73.

1987 *American Paradise: The World of the Hudson River School.* New York: The Metropolitan Museum of Art, p. 26.

1987 Menefee, Ellen Avitts. "The Early Biblical Landscapes of Thomas Cole (1825–1829)." Master's thesis, Rice University, pp. 33–40, 42, 47, 48, 50–53, 59, 61, 62, 64–70, 92.

1988 Parry, Ellwood C., III. *The Art of Thomas Cole: Ambition and Imagination.* Newark, London, and Toronto: University of Delaware Press, pp. 68–75, 77–83, 86, 89, 92–93, 114, 375, 383–385.

1990 Bolger, Doreen, and Kathleen Motes Bennewitz. "Thomas Cole's *Garden of Eden.*" *The Magazine Antiques* 128 (July): 105–111. (Color reproduction, pp. 104–105.)

1990 Parry, Ellwood C., III. "Thomas Cole's Early Drawings: In Search of a Signature Style." *Bulletin of the Detroit Institute of Arts* 66: 15–16, 17.

1990 Powell, Earl A., III. *Thomas Cole.* New York: Harry N. Abrams, pp. 42, 46, 47, 57, 96, 139.

1991 Parry, Ellwood C., III. "Les Montagnes dans L'Imaginaire de Thomas Cole." *Congres National des Sociétés savantes, Archaologie et histoire de l'art,* pp. 395, 397.

1992 Platt, Susan. "Paradigms and Paradoxes: Nature, Morality, and Art in America." *Art Journal* 51 (Summer): 82.

1992 Cash, Sarah. *American Art: Paintings from the Amon Carter Museum.* Fort Worth: Amon Carter Museum, pp. 10–11. (Color reproduction, p. 11.)

1993 Ketner, Joseph D. *The Emergence of the African-American Artist: Robert S. Duncanson, 1821–1872.* Columbia: University of Missouri Press, pp. 42–43.

1994 Truettner, William H., and Alan Wallach, eds. *Thomas Cole: Landscape into History.* New Haven and London: Yale University Press for National Museum of American Art, pp. 43, 45, 46, 79. (Color reproduction, p. 45.)

Compiled by LAURETTE E. McCARTHY